D1055372

POWER
– AND THE –
PEOPLE

Also by Alev Scott

Turkish Awakening: Behind the Scenes of Modern Turkey
Ottoman Odyssey: Travels Through a Lost Empire

POWER
— AND THE —
PEOPLE

THE ENDURING LEGACY OF
ATHENIAN DEMOCRACY

ALEV SCOTT AND
ANDRONIKE MAKRES

PEGASUS BOOKS
NEW YORK LONDON

POWER AND THE PEOPLE

Pegasus Books Ltd.
148 W 37th Street, 13th Floor
New York, NY 10018

Library of Congress Cataloging-in-Publication Data is available.

ISBN: 978-1-64313-562-5

10 9 8 7 6 5 4 3 2 1

Printed in the United States of America
Distributed by Simon & Schuster
www.pegasusbooks.com

Contents

Timeline of Athenian Democracy

ALL DATES ARE BC

461	Ephialtes' reforms (stripping the Areopagus of most of its powers)
454	Transference of the treasury of the Delian League from Delos to the Acropolis of Athens
451	Pericles' citizenship law
447	Work for the building of the Parthenon begins
431–404	Peloponnesian War
431	Funeral Oration delivered by Pericles
427	Mytilenian Debate
425	Performance of Aristophanes' *The Acharnians*
424	Performance of Aristophanes' *The Knights*
422	Performance of Aristophanes' *The Wasps*
416	Melian Dialogue
415	Launch of the Sicilian Expedition
406	Battle of Arginusae
404	Tyranny of the Thirty established in Athens by Sparta
403	Restoration of democracy
399	Death of Socrates
338	Battle of Chaeroneia – victory of Philip II of Macedon over Greek city states led by Athens and Thebes
336	Law against tyranny in Athens
334	Expedition of Alexander the Great begins
333	Statue of personified Demokratia dedicated in the Athenian Agora by the Council of Five Hundred

Note on Translations

Translations of Aeschylus, Aristophanes and Thucydides are by Jeffery S. Clackley, 2019. Unless otherwise stated, translations of other ancient sources and inscriptions are our own.

Note on Dates

The ancient year started in the summer, so each ancient year covered the second half of one year and the first half of the next, hence '505/504 BC'. We can only give a date as '505 BC' if we know the month of the historical event in question.

Introduction

The owl of Athena (symbol of wisdom), shown on
the reverse of Athenian silver coins of 5th century BC.

Democracy is feeling her age. It has been some time since she was honoured as a goddess, and even longer since she first appeared as an antidote to one-man rule. Today she is 'in crisis', in need of 'overhauling' or even 'rebooting', like an old computer. According to some political scientists, we will soon be living in a post-democratic world, once the Internet and ever-spiralling polarization have brought about her untimely demise. Others argue that technology is democracy's only hope, bringing power to the people's smartphones in a way that mimics the purer style of ancient direct democracy, saving us from the cranky old institutions we have begun to reject.

Before we get too alarmist, it is worth reminding ourselves that democracy has already disappeared and returned once (with a two millennia hiatus), and its essence has always been the same. *Demokratia* means the power (*kratos*) of the people (*demos*), a concept that was born in Athens at the end of the sixth century BC and flourished until 322 BC, when Macedonian rule forced the Athenians to dissolve their government and establish a plutocratic system in which only rich individuals could remain citizens. After this point, the institutions of democracy were resurrected in a weakened, zombie form, without the independence and freedom they once had. 'Demokratia' was used as a positive term for a few more centuries but it meant merely social stability, or cohesive society. The Roman Republic, despite its admiration for certain elements of Athenian society, regarded a democratic system of government as absurd, preferring the oligarchic constitution of Sparta.

Democracy effectively vanished from the world until the eighteenth century, when it returned in spirit with the revolutions in France and America, and developed with the republics that emerged from these revolutions. Direct democracy was still considered an outrageous idea, however, and the founding fathers of the United States of America chose to model their constitution on the Roman Republic rather than on Athens (although there is an increasingly fashionable theory that the United States' current superpower status is the modern incarnation of the Athenian Empire). Even after the formation of new republics and growing enfranchisement across Europe in the nineteenth century, the word 'democracy' was not really popularized until the early twentieth century. All too soon, it seems to be in danger of becoming obsolete.

If the first incarnation of democracy lasted around two hundred years, and we are now at the end of the two-hundred-year span of its second incarnation, the pessimistic among us might start preparing for the next hiatus. Or we might look back to work out how we can save democracy from crisis this time round. Nietzsche believed that 'we require history for life and action, not for the smug avoiding of life and action . . . Only so far as history serves life will we serve it.'[1] In other words, we should study history to the extent that it is useful to us; we can learn both from the mistakes and the successful innovations of democracy's ancient pioneers. Today, democracy is generally acknowledged as the best form of government, even though many of us are living in extremely flawed versions, and this assumption means there is not enough conversation about how to fix its flaws. Conversely, in ancient Athens there was vigorous debate about the best form of government – oligarchy (the rule of the few) versus democracy (the rule of the many) being the most contentious. Supporters of the latter had to actively defend and reinforce its legitimacy.

By ancient Athenian standards, the type of democracy many of us experience today is in fact an oligarchy. Many of us choose not to vote, usually through apathy, or a belief that our vote does not matter, and we have almost nothing to do with government. In effect, we are ruled indirectly by the minority of the electorate who vote for our representatives. In Athens, citizens voted on every decision, and a great proportion had an active role in government. The electorate was narrowly defined, yes – a problem we will come to – but power was firmly in their hands in a way that seems outrageously radical today.

The first section of this book explains how democracy came to be – the individuals who set up its institutions and legal safeguards, the egalitarian zeitgeist that powered it, and how it functioned in its initial form. The second section lays out five key lessons we can take from ancient Athens, and the third section examines cases of Athenian-style democracy making a comeback in the modern world – where it is working, where it is not, and where the trend might lead us. This is not a work of journalism or academia, but the product of a journalist and an academic swapping stories of cross-millennia politics and experiencing mutual déjà vu. We are certainly not the first to point out the parallels between modern democracy and its ancient form, though we are being more didactic than most in turning them into lessons. We feel the times demand it.

Our task has been made easier by the historian Thucydides, who picked democracy apart with a scalpel during the first century of its development. His account of the Peloponnesian War in 431–411 BC between the democratic Athenians and the oligarchic Spartans – a war in which he also fought – is indispensable to understanding the difficulties of sharing power, both then and now. He analysed the emerging psychology of the wisdom of the crowd in Athens, the concept of egalitarianism, the inevitable rise of demagogues and how a democratic power can become tyrannical overseas. He gave us probably the most famous definition of democracy to date, in the words of Pericles in 431 BC: 'Our constitution is called a democracy because power is in the hands not of the few but of the many.'

This definition has been employed either directly or indirectly by activists and poets throughout history, including Britain's Labour Party leader Jeremy Corbyn, who quoted 'The Mask of Anarchy', a poem by Percy Bysshe Shelley, to a crowd of supporters in London on 7 June 2017:

Rise like lions after slumber
In unvanquishable number –
Shake your chains to earth like dew
Which in sleep have fallen on you –
Ye are many, they are few.

It was a call to political arms that fell rather flat, but Pericles' words have inspired the many at least in theory, particularly in popular uprisings in the twentieth century as democracy made its great comeback. For the first few decades after democracy originally emerged in the sixth century BC, however, the concept of putting power in the hands of the people was not properly defined. 'Democracy' is still an elastic term today, so it is fitting that the word first appeared in disjointed form in one of the world's earliest theatrical works.

The Suppliant Women is a play by Aeschylus produced in the 460s BC, around fifty years after the foundations of democracy were laid in Athens. Aeschylus describes a vote taking place – totally anachronistically – in a mythical, non-Athenian kingdom. Nevertheless, he articulates the drama and beauty of collective decision-making; at one point in the play, the Chorus asks: 'Now tell us, to what end has the decision been ratified, and on which side are the hands of the people, by which they govern, more numerous?' The answer comes: 'The air bristled with right hands raised en masse, as they voted on this resolution.' The Greek expression used by Aeschylus – '*demou kratousa cheir*' – the governing hand of the *demos* – is a single image of the collective show of hands, a metaphor for democracy indicating the 'right' direction ('right hands held aloft').[2] The expression *demou kratousa cheir* almost forms the compound word *demokratia,* but not quite – that was yet to come. Modern Greeks still quote the following expression: 'With Athena's help, move your hand' – a legacy of the idea that Athena, goddess of wisdom and patron of the birthplace of democracy, guides people to act in their own best interests.

The lasting influence of Pericles' definition of democracy was foreseen by the man who committed them to history. At the beginning of his *History of the Peloponnesian War*, Thucydides predicts that the political events he catalogues will recur in similar form in the future, and explicitly dedicates his life's work to later audiences:

> *But if those who want to examine clearly the events that happened in the past, and which, given human nature, are likely to happen again, if they judge this work useful, that is enough. Rather than a show-piece meant to be heard for a moment, what is being composed here is a possession for all time.*[3]

While there is a certain amount of vanity in that statement, it is also true: human nature has remained the same, and Thucydides' work is still relevant, just as he predicted. Many of the same mistakes the Athenians made are being repeated; their crises re-emerge in different forms today. So it is a valid question to ask: what can we learn from them?

First, a caveat: in any comparison between ancient and modern democracy, we have to address the question of whether they are too different to be compared at all. For one thing, Athenian citizenship was far more exclusive than ours today. To be classed as a citizen from the middle of the fifth century BC onwards in Athens you had to be male, born from an Athenian father and an Athenian mother, and be above eighteen years old. Only this group of people, which represented around 20 per cent of the population, enjoyed the political rights and, crucially, the responsibilities of citizenship.

We may have a much broader electorate today, but only relatively recently. Women were given the vote in North America and most European countries only a hundred years ago (Greece didn't come round to the idea of female enfranchisement until 1952, and Switzerland until 1971), yet these countries were classed as democracies before that point. Throughout the 1960s in the United States, the civil rights movement fought to achieve the same voting rights for black people as were awarded to white people, and even today there is a legacy of unregistered black voters. Similar inequalities of citizenship awarded to foreigners still exist today as they did in ancient Athens – most countries operate a policy of taxation without representation, as the Athenians did with foreign residents not classed as citizens. Yet, even after admitting that our electorates are more inclusive than the Athenian prototype, we can draw useful parallels in how those electorates have worked over the millennia. Citizens' rights and responsibilities, the rule of law, foreign and domestic policy and the questions of how a democracy conducts an empire – all of these are not just interesting but vital comparisons to make in order to understand where and how our own democracies are going awry.

With those who argue that Athenian-style democracy could not be recreated today, we would agree. There is no way that the processes of direct and deliberative democracy that we explore in this book could be reproduced with the population sizes in most democratic states today – the Athenian model worked with tens of thousands of citizens, not millions. (Iceland is one of the closest contenders, with a population of around 350,000 and an appetite for deliberative democracy – see final chapter.) Modern democratic states could, however, be adapted more along ancient Athenian lines, with or without the aid of technology. The greatest thing missing today, which the Athenians had in spades, is a spirit of democratic engagement.

We have extraordinary levels of confusion and apathy within our modern electorates. We also have extraordinary levels of disgust and anger, and both reactions are to some extent the result of constant, invasive news cycles that previous generations did not have to deal with (calamities far more gruesome than disappointing referendum results – genocides, famines and wars – played out in relative secrecy before the advent of the Internet). Overwhelmed and confused, we disengage or get angry, which becomes polarizing.

Protest has become our preferred method of political engagement; protest movements are on the rise, globally, at the same time as voter turnout is falling, and it is more evident than ever that we are rejecting traditional democratic institutions. This is not all bad; the right to be heard is a vital ingredient of modern democracy, so at least it is being exercised. En masse, protesters can have the power to enact great change, but to be effective they rely on a common instinct to resist, and some kind of realistic expectation to achieve something. The last twenty years have seen large-scale protests with clear targets which have nonetheless failed, such as the London marches against the Iraq War (2002−3), alongside more visceral movements like the 2010−11 anti-austerity protests in Athens, a city where the democratic instinct to band together against the impositions of authority is hardwired and does not stand on ceremony. The protests of the Arab Spring, in which countless people died, tragically failed to achieve the democratic change they demanded.

Even when millions of angry people of different political stripes agree that, for example, negotiations for Britain's proposed exit from the European Union were unacceptably badly handled over the course of several years, the situation becomes so surreally normalized that protesting seems both inadequate and futile – like protesting against a natural disaster. Marches and petitions still happen, the civic pulse is there, but the incompetence of government can seem nebulous and terrifying, impossible to combat. It is difficult to know what to do, and protest only gets you so far. The crises our democracies are facing are much bigger than the single calamity of Brexit or the presidency of Trump, and they have the potential to get much worse. As the writer and film-maker Astra Taylor warns us: 'Democracy may not exist, but we'll miss it when it's gone.'

In 1820, Hegel wrote that 'The owl of Minerva [Greek Athena] only takes flight at dusk':[4] wisdom arrives too late for its era. This book is a very mortal attempt to catch a few stray feathers of Athenian wisdom before dark falls.

DEMOKRATIA:
The Life and Death of Athenian Democracy

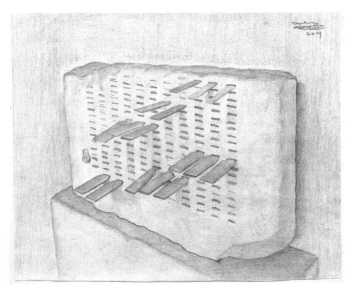

The *kleroterion*, an allotment machine for the appointment
of public officials. (Athenian Agora Museum)

Extreme Equality

Imagine a lottery ball machine, but for democracy. Under a reconstructed colonnade in the heart of Athens today, a slab of marble sits behind a sheet of glass. It looks as though it has been vandalized by a prisoner marking time – neat rows of identical indentations cover its surface. The effect is not attractive, and most tourists pass by with barely a glance. In the fourth century BC, this slab formed part of a machine, the *kleroterion*, that would have randomly selected citizens for public office. The machine stood in full view in the political centre of Athens so that everyone could see it in action – unlike the workings of democracy today.

We don't know who designed the *kleroterion*. Perhaps the idea was crowdsourced in true Athenian fashion, but some earnest individual or individuals came up with the idea of a stone democracy machine that ensured that selection for public office would be as fair as possible, a process known as sortition. A closer inspection of the marble reveals the methodical indentations to be slits into which bronze tags bearing the names of eligible candidates would have been inserted. Black and white balls would have been shaken from a bag into a funnel at the side of the slab, emerging haphazardly at the bottom of a tube. White meant yes, black meant no. Rows of the named tickets would be either accepted or rejected in turn – horizontally, vertically, diametrically or a combination – to select large numbers of names to serve in public office.

Unlike computers, *kleroteria* had the ancient advantage of being un-hackable, and sortition was used to pick people for almost every office except high positions in the military, for which a public vote based on the candidates' talent and reputation was thought to be a more sensible – and safer – system. The *kleroterion* slab on view today was found near the law court and would have been used for jury service, standing in front of the court and used at the last minute before a trial to prevent the possibility of the jurors being bribed. In the court, claimant and defendant represented themselves (although nothing prohibited their use of professional speech writers), and their time was limited with a water clock: a clay vessel with a plug at the bottom and a hole near the top to ensure exactly the same volume of water for everyone – another scrupulously fair, and un-hackable, contraption.

If the water clocks and the *kleroterion* were physical manifestations of equal opportunity and access to power, then *isonomia* (equality in front of the law) and *isegoria* (equal opportunity to speak in public) were the two major principles that underpinned democracy, much more so than today. Sole figures of authority were frequently objects of mistrust in Athens – a legacy from the days of tyranny that preceded the advent of democracy. There was no place for them, at least theoretically. There was no judge, only jurors in a court of law. There was no prime minister, or indeed any ministers at all, no official political parties and no electoral campaigns – people didn't choose their representatives, an indifferent machine did. Those picked by sortition for office would make decisions for a limited time – sometimes only a day, at most a year – before being replaced, and all proposed laws would be put to a public vote. In short, Athenian democracy at its best worked much more like today's jury system: you were plucked by chance to temporarily serve the state, rather than hustling your way into power as happens today – something that is inherently easier for richer, educated members of society. Universal access to public office without any preconditions was considered both a duty and a right for the Athenian electorate, the only way the system could function without the intermediaries we rely on today. Democracy made constant demands on citizens across the social spectrum who, one way or another, had to rise to the occasion.

System Abuse

Yet to err, as Alexander Pope reminds us, is human. The reason for the Athenians' strict rules regarding access to public office was that they understood all too well how self-interest naturally flourishes in any society if unchecked. People gravitate towards charismatic individuals, who accrue unofficial power that allows them to influence opinion. Unelected leaders compete. Cliques form, and opposition between them develops – organic political parties. Loyal supporters are favoured, pressure is brought to bear on rivals and before long, tribalism is in full working order, much as it is today with party politics.

Thucydides was fascinated by the way human nature takes any opportunity to cheat established laws; his description of the civil war in Corcyra (modern Corfu) in 427 BC could apply to any constitutional emergency in the modern world, any situation in which rules and normal democratic procedure break down. The horror of the Corcyran civil war may well have led Athens to introduce more checks and balances on its democracy in the fourth century.

With public life thrown into confusion, human nature, ever ready to rebel against the law, became the laws' master, gladly showed itself to be powerless over passion, stronger than justice and hostile to anything superior . . .

For party factions did not meet to enjoy the benefits of the existing laws, but for the advantage in overthrowing them. And the confidence that held these factions together was strengthened not by religious law rather but by their complicity in crime . . .

The cause of all these things was power based on greed and personal ambition.[1]

In ancient Athens, charismatic public speakers had a habit of becoming influential, hence the term 'demagogue'. *Ago* means to lead or drag – a demagogue [*demos* + *ago*] is by no means a noble 'leader of the people', but someone who drags them with sheer determination and ambition. Despite the reliance of the political system on random selection, Athenian society was in fact extremely meritocratic, and its competitive environment ensured the popularity of contests in public speaking as well as in athleticism (the Panathenaic contests) and theatre (the Dionysia), in which prizes were given to the best performers, playwrights and musicians. They were even awarded to particularly good orations in the law courts, so it is unsurprising that there was a market for demagoguery too. The public elections for high posts in the military meant that well-liked generals like Pericles and Alcibiades (champion of the disastrous attempt to invade Sicily in 415 BC) could influence the *demos* and essentially assume demagogic roles in the guise of military leaders (Pericles, for example, was chosen to be general fifteen years in a row, and dominated mid-century politics as a result).

Even in Athens, then, there was abuse of the political system despite the infrastructure that was so painstakingly built up to prevent it – an infrastructure which entailed time-consuming and expensive bureaucracy. Ostracism, the practice of voting to exile popular individuals who threatened the democratic equilibrium, had to be abandoned by the end of the fifth century BC, because, ironically, it had begun to be used as a tool by political adversaries to get rid of each other.

The *kleroterion* and system of rotation could only do so much, but they were, nonetheless, radical tools in allowing fair access to power, and tapping the fabled 'wisdom of the crowd'. Given the quality of many political representatives today, and the seemingly endless years they spend in power, it is difficult to argue that random group selection would be any worse than the quagmires modern citizens currently find themselves in – it might well be better. But current electorates would not adapt well to a sudden reversal to ancient standards of democracy. They have become accustomed to a lack of responsibility and an assumption that those in power will sort everything out, eventually – modern citizens are several steps removed from power, both in actuality and in our own estimation.

The Pnyx, where the Assembly of the Athenian people took place. The Acropolis can be seen in the background.

Voting in modern democracies is almost never mandatory (a few countries like Australia excluded); in ancient Athens, strict measures were taken to encourage attendance at the *ekklesia* or assembly, where citizens voted on issues from tax rates to foreign policy almost every week. We know from literary sources such as the comic playwright Aristophanes that slaves carrying ochre-stained rope corralled citizens in the city centre, the Agora, urging them up to the rocky plateau known as the Pnyx, opposite the central rocky hill of the city, the Acropolis. Here, the assembly would listen to the debates that took place – in which anyone could speak – before voting. A show of hands would determine which side held the majority; if it were not obvious, the votes would be counted individually, and it seems likely that a quorum of 6,000 was often the number of citizens required to be present at the assembly, as it was for ostracism (see Lesson Three). Anyone caught in the Agora with orange stains on their clothes (meaning they had lingered and been snagged by the ochre rope) would be fined. In Aristophanes' *The Acharnians,* there is a snide description of sluggish voters: 'Here's the fixed Assembly Day, and morning come, and no one in the Pnyx. They're gossiping away in the Agora, scurrying up and down to dodge the ochre-tinted rope.'[2]

Today, someone can vote in a referendum without being informed on the matter in any way; in ancient Athens, voters were forced to hear the arguments both for and against any motion. Human error and bias were just as possible then as now, of course, but at least the captive audience of voters resulted in a basically informed electorate.

Today, even those in power sometimes don't understand

the system that got them there. Electoral law is complicated. Although (some) governmental information is theoretically accessible to the public – for instance, via a Freedom of Information request – the process itself is unpublicized, seldom used and clumsily delivered. Mainstream and social media cloud the picture as much as they inform, and the result is that people are disassociated from the democracy in which they are theoretically involved. In ancient Athens, not only was the *kleroterion* in full view 24/7; so were written laws. Most new decisions taken by the public would be inscribed on a stone slab – *stele* – and set up on the Acropolis or in the Agora for all to read, like a billboard announcement which also served as a permanent record of the law. The spaces where these *stelai* were fixed into the rock are still visible on the Acropolis, if you know where to look. Trodden underfoot by legions of visitors climbing up to reach the Parthenon, they seem to be inexplicable, shallow indents – the graves of the world's first democratic decisions rubbed smooth and unremarkable by time.

The Acropolis

Ancient democracy manifests today as a series of spectacular tourist attractions awash with selfie sticks in the centre of Athens. The Agora is beautiful in its ruined state, but butchered: a wide open space with foundation stones and columns poking through the grass, right next to a railway that cuts through the centre of town. It was once at the heart of everything: the seat of government, a space for political debate, business and justice. The Panathenaic Way was a road leading through the Agora up to the Acropolis, designed originally for the religious procession up to the goddess Athena's temple, the Parthenon; it was also a political thoroughfare.

The architecture of the Parthenon has inspired the White House in Washington DC, the British Museum in London (where many of its ancient contents are controversially exhibited), and the logo of UNESCO – the temple of Athena remains the ultimate icon of global democracy today. From late antiquity onwards, Athena's temple was used as a church, then as a mosque, then as an armoury and gunpowder store by the Ottomans, blown up with a direct hit by the Venetians in 1687, and defaced by a Nazi flag under German occupation during the Second World War. Today, it is almost always covered in scaffolding (it is still – slowly – being restored after the Venetian explosion). The Acropolis is certainly not what it was, and one major absence is Athena, goddess of wisdom and the only authority the Athenians permitted to preside over democracy, who once loomed above her city in the form of a massive statue on the pinnacle of the hill.

Most Athenians today assume continuity between ancient Greece and modern Greece, but if you ask them what they associate with the Acropolis, answers are vague. Many say that the Parthenon is a symbol of democracy, and they are proud to live in its shadow, but they cannot quite articulate why. If pushed, some answer that it is a symbol of hope. They believe glory will return to the city in the future, and that at some point the Athens of today will be as great as the Athens of ancient times. Others feel that it's an oppressive symbol, a reminder of past achievement that is difficult to live up to – it has become something of a burden, particularly in the wake of the political and economic mess of the past decade. Put in cynical terms, it is an architectural beacon of Athens that serves primarily as a tourist attraction. The poet Giorgos Makris's 1940 surrealist manifesto: 'Proclamation No. 1',[3] which advocated blowing up the Parthenon in order to allow Athens to reinvent itself as a city free of ancient legacy, has recently come into academic vogue again.

But modern Athens has always had a slightly fractured relationship with its past. As you admire the view from the Agora towards the north of the city, away from the Acropolis, a graffiti-covered train thunders into view, cutting through the middle of the remains of the Altar of the Twelve Gods before disappearing into a tunnel which leaves visible only one corner of this venerated ancient relic. This altar was the heart of the Agora, and the central milestone from which all distances in Athens were calculated. Most of its foundations are hidden under the train line, and the story of its sole visible corner is a political parable worthy of Aesop – a study in how modern democracy can fail spectacularly, in the most inappropriate of settings, and the emotional toll of that failure.

Modern train crossing through the heart
of the ancient Athenian Agora.

In 2011, while repairs on the central Athenian metro were under way, state archaeologists took the opportunity to dig under the tracks. They unearthed for the first time the Altar of the Twelve Gods, a dramatic finding which was soon overshadowed by a bitter struggle between some of the archaeologists and the Greek state, the former arguing that the monument was too important to cover up again, the latter insisting that the Athenian public had a right to their repaired train line. Which should take precedence – the practical needs of the present or the symbolic importance of the past? In the words of a Greek academic who visited the dig:

What we saw surpassed by far what we expected, but we were told by the authorities that the monument would be covered again in a few days, so that the railway could be restored to its original track. Seeing all this and thinking about the fate of these extremely important antiquities made us feel ashamed and depressed. How can the Greeks be proud of their classical heritage and believe that Athenian democracy was the basis for modern democracies when they are not willing to figure out a way of diverting the railway? How is it possible that the Greek authorities are not willing to find a solution that would do justice to these exceptional antiquities? Why do we all let this happen?

The excavation of the Altar of the Twelve Gods received very little publicity, but those who were aware of it organized a protest at the site to stop the railway being built over the ruins. The angry archaeologists had unlikely allies in the form of the *dodekatheists*, a cult group who still believe in the twelve gods of the Greek mythical past, and who staged a hunger strike at the entrance of the Agora. The Thissio–Monastiraki line repairs were delayed, and the Athenian commuters waiting for their train line got more and more annoyed. In the end, a court decision ordered the repair work to resume; soon, the train line was functioning again and the Altar of the Twelve Gods was swallowed up, except for the corner poking out behind the wall of the railway, which is inside the archaeological site of the Agora. Another brutalized ruin run over by the train line is the foundations of the royal stoa, the seat of one of the three major archons responsible for religious matters. It was here that the philosopher Socrates was summoned for the crime of 'not believing in the gods of the state' in 399 BC – a transgression of democracy in its own right, as described later in this chapter.

In 2019, true to the cyclical and karma-heavy nature of Athenian tragedy, something the *dodekatheists* might consider the vengeance of the Twelve Gods struck the city. After many years of poor maintenance and natural erosion, parts of the Athenian tramline south of the city centre fell away, dramatically revealing the ancient River Illisos, on whose banks Socrates conducted the dialogues recorded by Plato. The river had been paved over during a period of urban development in the 1960s, surging under major avenues in central Athens ever since. Re-covering the river would cost millions, and the possible collapse of the eponymous Illisos Tunnel would effectively dam the river and flood Athens. Administrators were forced to consider rerouting the tramline to allow the river to be open to the elements again. The Twelve Gods were triumphant at last – perhaps.

This story brings to mind a less hopeful metaphor involving democracy and trains from the Mediterranean region. During his time as mayor of Istanbul in the mid-1990s, the democratically elected Recep Tayyip Erdoğan gave an honest preview of his future years of authoritarian-style presidency with a remark that has been widely quoted in the Turkish and English-language press, although it was delivered in the pre-Internet 1990s and has no written source: 'Democracy is like a train. Once you've reached your destination, you get off.'

How Democracy Began: A Crime Passionnel

The statues of Harmodius and Aristogeiton,
the tyrant-slayers of ancient Athens, who embodied
the notion of political freedom. (Museum of Naples)

Looking back at ancient Athens from the perspective of thousands of years, the picture can have a narrow, snapshot focus, because historians are understandably interested in the democratic golden years of Athens, and less in what preceded that. It is easy to believe democracy burst into life with a magnificent 'eureka' moment, a collective egalitarian instinct of the people, or perhaps a glorious revolution. In fact, its emergence, although relatively swift, was messy and non-linear – a rethinking of power, with a few brilliant individuals creating a legal framework to protect the new order.

But the original birth of democracy was something of an accident; it all started with a fatal love triangle.

In the sixth century BC, Athens was ruled by a tyrant named Peisistratus who passed power to his sons, much like the Assads of Syria. Peisistratus cut taxes for the poor and his regime, according to Aristotle, was 'more like a constitutional government than a tyranny'. He died of old age in 527 BC and his sons Hippias and Hipparchus took over. No serious complaints from the Athenians, many of whom were at that point already classed as 'citizens' as long as they belonged to one of the existing four tribes of kinship in Athens at the time. However, they had no real access to public office, which was hogged by the tyrants and their friends – again, like the Assads.

Then at some point before 514 BC, a young man caught Hipparchus' eye. Several ancient authors, Aristotle and Herodotus among them, dwell in detail on the salacious drama that followed. Here is Thucydides' account:

Harmodius was then in his youthful prime, and was the lover of Aristogeiton, a citizen of the middle class. Harmodius was propositioned by Hipparchus, son of Peisistratus, but he refused him and denounced him to Aristogeiton. But Aristogeiton, now the outraged lover, fearing Hipparchus' power and that he might take Harmodius by force, immediately plotted to overthrow the tyranny as best he could in his position. Meanwhile, Hipparchus again propositioned Harmodius, to no more success . . .[4]

Hipparchus, furious at being spurned, retaliated by humiliating Harmodius' sister at a public procession; the lovers, even more infuriated, were soon plotting their revenge with a few co-conspirators. At the Panathenaia festival (a special day when members of the public were allowed to carry arms) they armed themselves with daggers and approached Hipparchus in a panic, hoping that when they struck at their target, 'those not in on the plot would be carried away and . . . join in taking their liberty'.

Harmodius and Aristogeiton were wrong to assume that the Athenian public craved liberty enough to help them. The lovers 'immediately fell upon [Hipparchus] without hesitation, in all the fury that one, a man in love, the other a man humiliated, could feel . . .'

Harmodius was killed instantly by Hipparchus' bodyguard. Aristogeiton was captured, and tortured to give the names of the other conspirators. According to Aristotle's account, he was desperate to die; eventually, he tricked Hippias into holding his hand and then 'reviled Hippias for giving his hand to his brother's murderer. This enraged Hippias and, unable to control his anger, he pulled out his dagger and killed Aristogeiton.'[5]

The murder of Hipparchus led to seismic change: after his brother's murder, the embittered Hippias ruled with increasing cruelty and paranoia, contributing indirectly to the fall of his own tyranny by making himself unpopular enough to pave the way for a takeover. Four years later, a rival Athenian family brought down his brutal regime (by bribing the oracle of Delphi to divinely order the Spartans to help them), ultimately ushering in a softening of tyranny and the start of democracy. The 'Tyrant-Slayers' went down in Athenian history as defenders of political freedom, even as the founders of democracy, despite the fact that their act of murder was primarily a sexually motivated personal vendetta, exacerbated by fear of a lustful tyrant. As Thucydides rather cattily puts it, 'the Athenians themselves are no more accurate about their tyrants or their history'.

This creation myth of democracy was so strong in Athens that a special decree confirmed the tradition that 'the descendants of Harmodius and Aristogeiton, whoever is nearest in kin, should be granted permanent dining rights' – these rights referred to free dining in the Prytaneion, a state building in the Agora, which served the purpose of the seat of government. The lovers were also the first mortals to acquire statues in the Agora of Athens; the base of their statues was inscribed with verse by the poet Simonides: 'A marvellous shining light crowned Athens when Aristogeiton and Harmodius slew Hipparchus.'

Public statues have always had profound political significance. Today, we live in an age where left and right fight bitterly – sometimes literally – over the question of whether controversial figures such as Cecil Rhodes, the nineteenth-century British colonizer of Zimbabwe (previously Rhodesia), should remain standing in the University of Cape Town and in Oriel College, Oxford. In the US, a fatal protest movement erupted in 2017 over calls to remove the statue of Confederate soldier Robert E. Lee from the town of Charlottesville. Both movements have led to a rethinking of whether figures from the past deserve a public place in the present, and there is an uneasy hiatus in place; the Confederate statue, for example, is now covered in a black shroud which is periodically removed by right-wing protesters, and replaced by town authorities. Harmodius and Aristogeiton were venerated as murderers with a righteous cause; they have not been reinterpreted through the lens of history, and they will not be covered by a shroud – they are too archaic, safe in the distant past. Instead, their act of violence will always be remembered as the catalyst for an era of unprecedented political freedom.

Feminine Democracy

Law against tyranny, with a relief of Democracy,
shown as a young woman, crowning Demos,
an old man personifying the people of Athens.
(Athenian Agora Museum)

33

The tyrant-slayers may have been male, but the real icons of Athenian democracy were female. In the fourth century BC, more than a hundred years after the tyrant-slayers' death, Demokratia (a noun in the feminine gender in Greek) began to be depicted as a beautiful young woman, and then as a goddess – fitting, given Athens' eponymous goddess, Athena. But Demokratia's womanly incarnation is also ironic, given that women were not allowed to vote in ancient Athens, and to a modern eye, there is an obvious dichotomy between the public worship of a goddess and the lack of female suffrage. One particularly absurd manifestation of this is a public prosecution that dates from around the time of the deification of Demokratia, of a citizen called Lykophon, who was accused of having an affair with an Athenian woman. He was charged with the attempted corruption of a freeborn Athenian woman (citizen), a crime deemed an attack on democracy itself, and tantamount to treason. Meanwhile, in *Lysistrata*, by Aristophanes, the women of Athens bring an end to war by staging a sex strike – an effective act of political protest.

The creation myth of democracy revolves entirely around women. According to the first-century BC Roman author Varro (in a story retold by the monk St Augustine in the early fifth century AD), the goddess Athena (Roman Minerva) and the god Poseidon (Roman Neptune) competed for the city of Athens at its foundation. Athena offered its first inhabitants an olive tree and Poseidon a salt sea spring. On consulting the oracle at Delphi, the Athenians decided to vote for which deity they wanted:

When the multitude consulted, the men gave their votes for Nep-
tune, the women for Minerva; and as the women had a majority
of one, Minerva conquered. Then Neptune, being enraged, laid
waste the lands of the Athenians, by casting up the waves of the
sea; for the demons have no difficulty in scattering any waters
more widely. The same authority said, that to appease his wrath
the women should be visited by the Athenians with the threefold
punishment – that they should no longer have any vote; that none
of their children should be named after their mothers; and that no
one should call them Athenians.[6]

In other words, women outvoted men in the first ever
referendum, and their punishment was to be immediately
and forever disenfranchised – even though the beneficiary of
their vote, the goddess Athena, continued to be worshipped
for centuries to come. While the hypocrisy of the Athenian
attitude towards women and democracy is painfully apparent
2,500 years on, it is a misconception that women had no
significant place in Athenian society. The long-standing view
that they were shut up in their homes and could only see the
world if they were engaged in some religious activity or if
they were working as prostitutes is being increasingly challenged. Despite Poseidon's injunction that 'no one should call
[women] Athenians', they were counted as citizens because
citizenship involved not only political rights but inheritance
rights, a role in ancestral rites, and in religion (priesthood was
a state office, so priestesses were public servants). Traditional

scholarship has assumed that a female flute player depicted on a vase would have been a prostitute, but now, scholars acknowledge that she would more likely have been a professional flute player. This theory is being confirmed by archaeologists who have re-examined votive offerings to the gods on the Acropolis, bearing inscriptions from women who dedicated these objects worth 10 per cent of their earnings. Women undoubtedly worked – to give one well-known example, Aristophanes made fun of the mother of the great tragedian Euripides, because she was a lettuce-seller. The presence and power of so many female goddesses and literary personae in Athenian drama and prose, moreover, would suggest that women were prominent in the non-political life of the city – just as Swiss women were in Swiss society before 1971.

In 336 BC, the Athenians passed a pre-emptive law against tyranny, and on its famous *stele* the text is accompanied by an illustration of the beautiful Demokratia crowning an old man, Demos (a personification of the people of Athens). Around this time, the Athenians also set up a colossal statue of Demokratia in the form of a female goddess, like an ancient prototype of the Statue of Liberty. The inscription is preserved and reads as some kind of self-congratulatory pat on the back by the Council of Five Hundred for being 'virtuous and just':

> *DEMOKRATIA. In the year when Nikokrates was archon [333/2 BC] the Council of Five Hundred dedicated [this statue], having been crowned by the People for its virtue and justice.*

The personification of democracy and its subsequent deification is not easy to date but would have been after democracy was restored to Athens with the expulsion of the oligarchic regime imposed on the city by Sparta in 404 BC, after the latter won the Peloponnesian War; their rule lasted barely eight months. The cult of Demokratia seems to have been at its height in the second half of the fourth century BC; around the same time, 'Demokratia' started to appear as a baby name for Athenian girls and even for triremes (warships), a sign of the political system embedding itself firmly into popular culture. It is striking that in the same year that the Demokratia goddess statue was erected (333 BC), Alexander the Great, posing as a liberator rather than as a conqueror, was removing pro-Persian oligarchies in the Greek cities of Asia Minor and replacing them with democracies (Alexander at that time happened to be on particularly good terms with Athens).

As its cultural influence spread, democracy itself began to lose its spontaneity. It became more bureaucratic and institutionalized as time passed from its radical inception in the late sixth century: the cult of the goddess Demokratia, for example, was formalized, as scholars know from a third-century stone seat in the Theatre of Dionysus, which bears an inscription stating that the seat was reserved for 'the Priest of Demokratia'. There is also epigraphic evidence that Athenian generals sacrificed to Demokratia before battle, an image that brings to mind the icons of the Virgin Mary in chapels on Greek navy boats and in other military contexts today; the armed forces have always employed religion as a kind of insurance policy, be it pagan or church. The masculine version of Demokratia – *Demokrates* – had already begun to appear as a baby name for Athenian boys at the end of the fifth century BC, as well as a wide range of names which are *demos-* compounds – the most famous being Demosthenes ('Strength of the People'), the great statesman of the fourth century BC. Just as democracy had fully embedded itself in Athenian culture as something to be worshipped, celebrated and preserved, it faced its demise.

The cult of Demokratia was 150 years down the line from the birth of democracy in the late sixth century BC, and the tyrant-slayers Harmodius and Aristogeiton were only accidental heroes. There were others – peaceful philosophers and military leaders among them – who did the real work of transforming Athens into a democracy, often at cost to themselves. Two major players who did the constitutional legwork were Solon and Cleisthenes.

Heroes of the Sixth and Fifth Centuries BC

Solon

In 1889, some dog-eared rolls of papyrus were acquired by the British Museum. Tedious financial accounts from around AD 78 were written on one side of them, but on the back something much more interesting was identified by the scholar

F. G. Kenyon on 26 February 1890: it was a copy of Aristotle's *Athenian Constitution*, a text of the second half of the fourth century BC known and referred to throughout antiquity but lost to the modern world – until now. The discovery, which was made public in *The Times*, on 19 January 1891, took the world of classical scholarship by storm. Aristotle, or perhaps one of his pupils, had recorded step by step the formation of democracy and the resulting constitution.

The surviving story begins at the end of the seventh century with Draco – the fierce disciplinarian responsible for our English word 'draconian' – who wrote Athens' first set of laws. His law on homicide, which contains the seminal distinction between premeditated and unpremeditated murder, was the only law which survived subsequent revisions by Solon. One of the seven sages of antiquity, Solon was hated and honoured in equal measure when he attempted to fix Athens' broken society by scaling back the vast inequality between rich and poor. In the early sixth century BC, when he implemented his reforms, the constitution of Athens was aristocratic – the 'power [*kratos*] of the best [*aristos*]' – meaning that legislative, deliberative and executive power was in the hands of members of aristocratic families, the so-called well born. There were nine magistrates known as the nine archons, and a High Court justice body called the Areopagos which was the 'guardian of the laws', whose lifelong members were composed of ex-archons.

Poor Athenian citizens were often in debt to wealthy ones and would be effectively enslaved if they failed to pay their debts. It was this social crisis that led the Athenians, with an admirable degree of self-reflection, to appoint Solon as an arbitrator to solve their problems. He operated like a doctor ministering to a patient (a metaphor beloved of ancient Athenians – see Nicias in Lesson Three of this book); he had spotted the cause of the disease – the greediness of the wealthy and the stripping of the dignity of the poor – and he knew how to cure it.

So in 594 BC, long before the overthrow of the Peisistratid tyranny, Solon embarked on a programme of ambitious reform: he abolished citizen slavery, cancelled both private and public debts, changed the criterion for election to public office from high birth to wealth, created the Council of the Four Hundred, and established the popular law courts and the right of appeal. His reforms were so powerful – and controversial – that soon after he implemented them he went into self-imposed exile to have some peace from his critics: 'I turned about like a wolf among many dogs,' he complains in one of his confessional poems.

Solon had managed to annoy the entire spectrum of Athenian society. Rich landowners would now miss out on money owed to them after Solon cancelled debts, and would also miss their 'debt slaves'. But impoverished Athenians were also indignant because they had hoped for a redistribution of land, which Solon did not do. In fact, he was – theoretically – in favour of minimal intervention.

I gave to the people as much privilege as is sufficient for them
Not detracting from their dignity or reaching out to take it,

And to those who had power and were admired for their wealth
I declared that they should suffer nothing unseemly.
I stood holding my mighty shield against both,
And did not allow either to win an unjust victory.[7]

So in the end, Solon the grandiose centrist left Athens to a hail of abuse and the social crisis was not fully resolved, providing fertile ground for Peisistratus, a charismatic aristocrat, to gain support using populist methods and to establish illegitimate one-man rule (tyranny): a paradigm for our times. It is ironic, in fact, that both the heroes and the anti-heroes of early Athenian democracy – men like Peisistratus and Cleisthenes – were all aristocrats.

Solon's laws had a relatively weak short-term effect but a colossal long-term one. The rule of law became sovereign, a pivotal moment in the history of democracy. What is remarkable is how publicly accessible both his and Draco's laws were, inscribed on physical objects (*axones* and *kyrbeis*) that stood on the Acropolis for around 150 years, before being brought down to the Agora. The *axones* on which the laws of Solon were inscribed were large, cuboid pieces of wood mounted in an oblong frame, so that Athenians could read the text inscribed on each of the four flat surfaces by turning the wood.

The physically inscribed laws of Solon set a precedent for the legal constitutions we have today. Almost all modern states have had revolutions or been granted independence at some point, and so have codified constitutions, such as the United

States, whose constitution is treated today with near-biblical reverence. There are one or two other countries that haven't: Canada (partly codified), New Zealand (likewise), Saudi Arabia and, rather surprisingly, Israel. The British constitution is an exception; nobody ever sat down and designed it, much as no one designed English common law. Instead, it developed in a piecemeal fashion over a millennium or more.

The Athenian constitution was largely codified, but some of Solon's laws were more explicit than others, and Aristotle considers the theory that he deliberately made some of them open to interpretation in a bid to keep democracy on its toes – 'in order that the power of decision should rest with the people'; he ultimately concluded, however, that not everything can be codified because it is simply 'impossible to define what is best in general terms'. Sometimes it is even less possible to define what is best in specific terms; in the wake of recent mass shootings in the US, for example, the debate over the right to bear arms – enshrined in the American constitution – shows that some laws just do not age well.

Cleisthenes

In 510 BC, after the Spartans' overthrow of the final tyrant, Hippias (brother of the spurned Hipparchus), there was literal anarchy in Athens. 'Anarchy' originally meant 'the archon-less year' – in other words, no archon or legitimate senior magistrate in charge, which has been effectively the case in

Britain since the 2016 referendum – Boris Johnson's embry-onic premiership notwithstanding. In both cases, the situation was not ideal, but just about tolerable, and in 508 BC, the great visionary Cleisthenes fortunately took the reins in Athens.

We date the birth of democracy not from Solon's laws but from Cleisthenes' reforms of 508, which he implemented less than twenty years before the Battle of Marathon, a victory for the Athenians over an invading Persian force. Cleisthenes created the Council of Five Hundred from Solon's Council of the Four Hundred, stipulating that its citizen members had to be above the age of thirty, and could serve only twice in their lifetime. He also introduced ostracism. But his most transformative idea was to redraw electoral zones in the state of Athens and artificially create tribes that spanned these zones, thus uniting unconnected people and enforcing a sense of the *demos* as a whole, something bigger and more important than private interest or loyalties of kinship.

This was more radical than it sounds – Cleisthenes invented what we today call stratified sampling (the process which ensures that different segments of a population are proportion-ately represented in a random selection) by transforming the democratic geography of Athens. Before Cleisthenes, a tribe was a segment of the population divided according to kinship (real or assumed); after his reforms, it became a segment divided according to geography. It is a common misconception that ancient Athens corresponded to the modern city. Politically speaking it was in fact the entire state of Attica, stretching from the port of Piraeus and the temple of Sounion in the south, to the temple of Artemis in Vravrona on its eastern coast and Eleusis in the west. This coastal, agricultural and urban landscape was divided by Cleisthenes in such a way as to ensure every area was represented by an equal number of randomly selected citizens on a council of 500; every year, the members of the council were selected afresh. Any preliminary decision proposed by this council would then have to survive a public vote at the Assembly, which convened around forty times a year.

In a stroke of genius, Cleisthenes redrew the political map of Athens – in an age before maps existed – to create a sense of solidarity between people who would otherwise have relatively little in common. First, he divided the land of Attica into three zones (*trittyes*): the coast, the inland region and the city centre, each of which was made up of demes, like boroughs. Then, he divided all the Athenian citizens of Attica into ten tribes, which is where it gets interesting. In order to create loyalties between the people from all three *trittyes*, Cleisthenes made sure that the make-up of each of the ten tribes was a mix of members of demes from all three zones (coast, inland and city centre). If the total Athenian electorate was roughly 50,000 (representing perhaps 20 per cent of the entire population), then each tribe would have comprised approximately 5,000 citizens. Of the 500 chosen each year to be on the Council, approximately one-third would be members of demes that were from the coast, another third from demes that were located inland and the

44

last third would be from demes that were located in the urban centre. All the demes of Attica had at least one representative (and more than one if the deme had a large population) who became a member of the Council of Five Hundred, and the mix was intended to ensure that no single local interest had a disproportionate voice, and that different regional voices were forced to compromise for the common good when serving on the Council. Aside from involvement in central administration, citizens were also constantly involved in the local assembly meetings of their own demes, and election of local magistrates. (see image on p. 66)

Cleisthenes was, in a way, a reverse Stalin, who deliberately created divisions in Soviet territory in the 1920s by redrawing political lines in Central Asia, so that people of different ethnic and religious backgrounds would be at loggerheads – a classic policy of divide and conquer. Cleisthenes did the opposite – by connecting geographically separated people, he created a new kind of kinship and ensured equal representation.

Post-Cleisthenes

What was still missing in Athenian democracy after Cleis-thenes' reforms was the empowerment of the middle and lower classes (strictly defined according to their wealth), and the fact that the elitist Areaopagus (composed of ex-archons) continued to exercise too many powers, like the House of Lords in Britain. In the context of Greek city states, military success often translated into political power, so the empowerment of the middle and lower classes came about from an exterior threat: the invading Persians in the early fifth century BC. A few years after the Battle of Marathon (a victory for Athens due to the hoplites, or foot soldiers, who were members of the middle class), the general Themistocles created the Athenian fleet which eventually won the naval battle of Salamis in 480 BC against the Persians who were invading Greece for a second time. The victory at the Battle of Salamis empowered the rowers who were members of the lowest social class (the *thetes*), just as the hoplites had been empowered ten years earlier; as soon as the Persian danger was gone, there was a notable impetus towards democracy. In some ways, the full enfranchisement of the hoplites and rowers in recognition of their service mirrors the move towards granting women the vote in European democracies after their participation in the First World War.

More practical contributions to democracy came in the wake of Themistocles during the fifth century BC. Ephialtes abolished most of the powers of the aristocratic council of the Areopagus in 461 BC – for some, this is the real date that democracy began. Ten years later, Pericles brought democracy into its radical form. He introduced citizenship law, payment for public office, funds to pay for the poor to attend the theatre, and gave what came to be a formative definition of democracy in the Funeral Oration recorded by Thucydides, delivered in 431 BC in honour of those who had died in the first year of

46

the Peloponnesian War. (Soon afterwards, Athens was hit by a plague which claimed the life of Pericles himself.)

For we have a system of government that does not emulate the institutions of our neighbours, making us more an example to some rather than leading us to imitate others. It is called a democracy because power is in the hands not of the few but of the many. In accordance with the laws private disputes are equal; in accordance with each man's recognition is he singled out for public service; and never on account of poverty is someone who can do good for the state prevented from doing so by the obscurity of their background.

In public life we conduct ourselves with freedom, and so also in our private life, and we don't look suspiciously towards our neighbours' everyday habits, nor get angry about it, or even cast those dirty looks that do no harm but nonetheless cause offence.

Though we enjoy ease in our private life we are especially law-abiding in our public life because of respect, namely an unswerving obedience to those in office and to the laws, especially to those laws – written and unwritten – that protect the wronged and cannot be broken without bringing universal condemnation.[8]

The speech was intended to be morale-boosting at a time when Athenians would have been frightened and grieving at the outbreak of war, perhaps doubting whether democracy was worth fighting for. Pericles emphasized democracy's all-embracing qualities, how it affords the same access to power and legal protections to rich and poor, and promotes tolerance for those who adopt a different way of life from the majority. Yet there was an edge to this speech: Pericles was claiming Athenians were superior to other Greeks because of their sensitivity in observing egalitarian principles – Athens, according to him, was 'a model for others'. There is more than a hint of this moral superiority in the speeches of modern democratic leaders; President Kennedy, for example, on his visit to West Berlin in 1963 during the Cold War, pointed out that: 'Freedom has many difficulties and democracy is not perfect, but we have never had to put a wall up to keep our people in, to prevent them from leaving us.' Democracy has always engendered in its champions a kind of evangelism.

Twelve Hundred Angry Men:
a case study in justice

The mythical origins of the Athenian justice system are outlined in the final play of the *Oresteia*, the trilogy of bloody family tragedies written by Aeschylus in the fifth century BC. In *The Eumenides*, Orestes, who has killed his mother in revenge for her killing of his father, is pursued by the Furies, terrifying goddesses of vengeance, but is finally granted a trial by Athena. The jury of twelve is split, until the goddess herself casts her vote in favour of sparing him. The assumption of innocence which underlies modern justice systems stems from this vote of mercy, as well as the play's coda: Athena transforms the feared Furies into merciful 'Eumenides' – 'kindly ones' – to symbolize the superiority of a democratic justice system over privately motivated revenge. The story also explains why there were always odd numbers of jurors in ancient Athens, so that votes could not be evenly split – a simple majority would decide the defendant's fate (as opposed to modern juries of twelve, where a unanimous verdict is required in most cases, or at best at 10−2 majority – anything else is classed as a hung jury, in England at least, necessitating a retrial).

In 1954, the American playwright Reginald Rose wrote *Twelve Angry Men*, a play (and later film) that explores the terrifying responsibility of a jury, the extent to which prejudice can influence individuals, and how a charismatic individual can change the tide of opinion. The plot follows a jury deliberating over the fate of a Puerto Rican teenager accused of murdering his father; all of the twelve jurors (who are male, the norm in the US until after 1973 when women were allowed to serve on juries in all fifty states) initially assume he is guilty apart from one. This rogue juror introduces 'reasonable doubts' into the minds of the other men, forcing them to confront their narrow-minded reasons for leaping to a guilty verdict. The play is chilling, if you look at it as a portrait not of justice but of psychological influence: one individual can persuade an entire jury of his particular point of view, whatever that might be.

Although modern juries mimic the Oresteian model of twelve, Athenian juries numbered at least 501 for public cases, often more, and at least 201 for private cases. The meanings of 'public' and 'private' in Athenian society are contentious distinctions among scholars, but broadly speaking, public concerned the *polis* (state); anything else would have been classed as private. For example, the murder of a citizen in public office, however minor their role, would usually be classed as a public crime, whereas the murder of someone's cousin in a row over inheritance would be classed as private. The annual pool of jurors, whose official name was Heliaia, numbered 6,000. Several of the law courts were in the area of the Agora, where excavations by American archaeologists have unearthed a ballot box which contained one small bronze ball used for the allotment machine (*kleroterion*), described at the beginning of this chapter, that now stands behind glass in the reconstructed colonnade, the Stoa of Attalus.

As one might expect from the people who came up with the *kleroterion*, the design of Athenian ballots was also ingeniously fair. Six jurors' ballots were found in the Agora excavations; the hub of the ballot indicated the verdict, solid for an acquittal and hollow for a conviction, so that if the juror covered with his forefinger the ends of the hub he could deposit his vote in secrecy. This is an important distinction from modern juries of twelve, where discussion is part of the procedure of collective decision-making, as demonstrated in Rose's play. In Athens, every one of the hundreds of jurors made up their own minds singly and privately. Here is Aristotle's description of the procedure:

There are bronze ballots, with an axle through the middle, half the ballots are hollow and half solid. When the speeches have been made, the men appointed by lot to take charge of the ballots give each juror two ballots, one hollow and one solid, in full view of the litigants so that no one shall take two solid or two hollow . . . There are two jars in the court, one of bronze and one of wood . . . The jurors cast their votes in these: the bronze jar counts and the wooden does not; the bronze one has a pierced attachment through which only one ballot can pass, so that one man cannot cast two votes. When the jurors are ready to vote, the herald first makes a proclamation, to ask whether the litigants object to the testimonies: objections are not allowed once the voting has begun. Then he makes another proclamation: 'The hollow ballot is for the litigant who spoke first (prosecutor), the solid for the one who spoke afterwards (defendant).' The juror takes his ballots together from the stand, gripping the axle of the ballot and not showing the contestants which is the hollow and which is the solid, and drops the one that is to count into the bronze jar and the one that is not into the wooden.[9]

Because of random juror sortition, juries would probably have reflected a wide spectrum of different social classes, at least until Pericles introduced jury pay of two obols in the 430s (later increased to three obols by the demagogue Cleon), which suggests that poorer citizens were encouraged to participate in the jury courts. In fact, ancient writers like the comedian Aristophanes imply that jury service played the role of a benefits system, which poor citizens came to rely on as a source of income, as well as a daily power trip.

Aristophanes was a fierce satirist – the *Private Eye* writer of his day, but much more wicked. He is one of the best sources of information about Athens' political and social life of the fifth century BC. His play *The Wasps* features a chorus acting like a swarm of wasps – the jurors of Athens, ever buzzing around the law courts, both annoying and dangerous. Procleon is an old man addicted to jury service, thinking it elevates him. Contracleon, his son, tries to get him to overcome this addiction and to understand that jury service is actually exploitation of the jurors rather than the other way round. The names of Procleon and Contracleon are wordplays on the real-life demagogue Cleon, much villainized by Aristophanes throughout his work.

There are several jokes in *The Wasps* about jurors being reluctant to acquit or grant light sentences – Procleon suffers a breakdown after he is persuaded to acquit someone. Athenian jurors drew a line in a wax tablet to indicate the length of sentence they thought the condemned man should receive, so Procleon, predictably, is discovered to have huge amounts of wax embedded under his fingernails, indicating a thirst for long sentences. At one point, he gives a speech in which he lists his favourite perks as a veteran juror:

> *Here and now, I will make a proof of our power, how it is equal to any royal sovereignty. For is there now a creature more happy or more blessed than a juror, or more spoiled or more terrifying,*

even though he's just an old man? As soon as I get up from my bed, great and lofty men are waiting for me on the courthouse steps: and then just as I approach, one of them offers me his hand, soft from embezzling public funds: they act the suppliant, bowing and pouring out their piteous pleas.[10]

We wouldn't laugh at Aristophanes' jokes unless we recognized the truth in them – he captured something evergreen about the nature of power, and the gullibility of the public. The freedom to write political satire is a cornerstone of democracy, one that is threatened when democracy itself is threatened. Academic freedom is another cornerstone that can be attacked from both left and right, as we have seen happen at various points throughout the last hundred years. In ancient Athens, the freedom of philosophers to operate without interference from the state varied over the fifth and fourth centuries BC; their story is a valuable lesson for our times.

Hell-Bound Philosophers:
a case study in academic freedom

It is easy to get lost while walking on Filopappou Hill, just opposite the Acropolis. Olive trees and bright-yellow forsythia flank paths onto which tortoises occasionally emerge – a bucolic mirage that belies its location right in the centre of Athens. Most people head straight up to the hill's rocky apex to see the Acropolis, or look down at the cityscape stretching down towards Piraeus harbour.

But hidden in one of the olive groves is a series of caves built into the rock. Locals believe these were the cells of the prison where Socrates was held – an impression deepened by the bars that cover the entrances to the caves, a modern security measure that also entices tourists to the spot (despite the fact that it is unlikely to be the real site of Socrates' incarceration). Socrates' works were never written down, but two of his pupils, Plato and Xenophon, recorded his relentless questioning of perceived wisdom and methods of philosophical interrogation – he was perhaps the first great intellectual celebrity to speak truth to power. When he served a term on the board of the *prytaneis* (the presiding committee composed of fifty members of the Council of Five Hundred) he went against the rest of the board members on a point of principle, as we will explore in the next chapter. He did not believe in the wisdom of the ordinary man, and acted as the 'gadfly' of Athens, in Plato's words, annoying powerful men by pointing out the illogic of anything they said, and challenging lazy assumptions about both private and public ethics. Nevertheless, he believed so vehemently both in the rule of law and in speaking what he thought to be the truth that he died when those beliefs clashed. In a sense, democracy killed him.

After their victory in the Peloponnesian War in 405/404 BC, the Spartans abolished democracy in Athens and established a bloody oligarchy later known as the 'Thirty Tyrants', a puppet government composed of specially chosen Athenians with oligarchic sympathies. Socrates was tainted by association with this regime because one of the most prominent of the Thirty Tyrants, Critias, was a former pupil of his; another famous ex-pupil, the general Alcibiades, had defected to Sparta. In 399 BC, just four years after the Thirty Tyrants were deposed and democracy restored in Athens, Socrates was put on trial. Democracy seemed to be in a fragile state and Athenians were jumpy. Socrates, who was by then a well-known critic of the establishment, was tried for the crime of 'corrupting the minds of the youth of Athens and of not believing in the gods of the state'. This was of course an excuse; the real reason was most likely his mentorship of oligarchs and general unpopularity.

During his defence, Socrates predicted that his conviction would be the outcome, not through a fair trial but because he was a popular hate figure and the jurors disliked him. This point bears relevance to modern rules prohibiting jurors from googling the names of the defendants they are trying – if a jury is not open-minded, the entire concept of justice collapses.

> But you may be assured that what I said before is true, that great hatred has arisen against me and in the minds of many persons. And this it is which will cause my condemnation, if it is to cause it, not Meletus or Anytus [Socrates' accusers], but the prejudice and dislike of the many. This has condemned many other men who are also good.[11]

Socrates was convicted, as he expected. When asked to suggest his own sentence, he argued that he should be rewarded for his years of service to the state (meaning not his military service during the Peloponnesian War or service as a *prytanis*, but his scrutiny of public and private morals); instead, he was sentenced to drink hemlock. Both Xenophon and Plato tell us that he was given the chance to escape after his friends bribed the prison guards, but he refused.

If Socrates were alive today, his story would be less dramatic; he would perhaps take the form of some public intellectual lambasted on social media for politically incorrect views. Some of his ideas might cause genuine offence, but others might be pounced upon simply because they were the wrong things to say at the wrong time. A tipping point would be reached, when it would no longer be acceptable to defend him at social gatherings or in a newspaper column even if, privately, you thought what he said was not so bad after all, or even if you *did* think what he said was bad, but felt the punishment did not fit the crime. His words would be weaponized and turned back on him, just as they were at the turn of the fourth century BC, and his hemlock would be a social lynching.

Before his death, Socrates had already established a philosophical dynasty. His method of teaching – wandering around the city and interrogating strangers as his acolytes followed behind – was copied in a more entrepreneurial format by his pupils. Although Socrates never accepted payment, the freelance philosophers who followed him began to hold regular open-air seminars of their own, charging those who attended. By the end of the fourth century, four major philosophical schools of Athens were established: the Academy, founded by Plato; the Peripatos (school of the 'peripatetics', or those who walked around), founded by Aristotle (a pupil of Plato, and thus an indirect pupil of Socrates); the Garden of the philosopher Epicurus, founder of Epicureanism; and the Stoic School of Zeno, so called because his classes met by the Stoa in the Agora. Plato was an Athenian, and Epicurus had Athenian parents although he himself was born on the island of Samos, but the other two founders of the philosophical schools were metics, or foreign residents of Athens (Aristotle was from Stageira in Macedon, and Zeno from Kitium in Cyprus).

These philosophical schools, the first truly academic institutions, were private initiatives, theoretically outside state control. However, in the year 307 BC, the Assembly passed a paralysing censorship decree that was, in the words of a comic poet of the time, 'a law that sent the philosophers to hell'. The wording was as follows: 'It should not be possible for any philosopher in a school to speak unless the Council and the Assembly have so decided. Otherwise the penalty be death.' The justification was that these philosophical schools corrupted the young, but, as with the charge against Socrates, this was an excuse – the real reason was political, linked to the support given to Aristotle's Peripatos school by the recently departed Athenian ruler Demetrius, a puppet of Macedon and himself a peripatetic. All the philosophers left Athens in protest – a development so appalling that public opinion quickly changed. Not only was the law overturned, the man who had proposed it was convicted by an overwhelming majority of the crime of 'making an illegal proposal', and the philosophers soon returned. Ironically, academic freedom had been strengthened by this episode, which criminalized state interference in the schools, and Athens remained a bastion of learning and free speech well after its golden age of democracy – a legacy that continues today. The last line of a famous motto of the ancient orator Isocrates now stands inscribed above the doors of the Gennadius Library of the American School of Classical Studies in Athens:

And so far has our city distanced the rest of mankind in thought and in speech that her pupils have become the teachers of the rest of the world; and she has brought it about that the name Hellenes [Greeks] suggests no longer a race but an intellect, and that the title Hellenes is applied rather to those who share our culture than to those who share a common blood.

The twentieth century is full of examples of persecuted thinkers – the scientists and university professors driven out of Germany by the Nazis in the 1930s, for example, or the Eastern European philosophers forced to flee west by Communist regimes – and the pattern is still playing out in the twenty-first century. Turkey is an example of a country increasingly hostile to free thought, and in particular to academics; in a public speech in January 2016, President Erdoğan lambasted the 1,128 academics who signed a 'peace petition' calling for an end to the conflict between Turkish troops and Kurdish militants in south-east Turkey. 'This crowd, which calls itself academics, accuses the state through a statement,' he said. 'Hey, you so-called intellectuals! You are not enlightened persons, you are dark. You are nothing like intellectuals.'[12] After the coup of July 2016, some of those academics – who had effectively signed their own arrest warrant with the petition – were imprisoned on charges of treason; many of the others left the country to avoid the same fate and there is currently a considerable community of Turkish writers and intellectuals adrift in Europe.

It goes without saying that a mass exodus of intellectuals does not bode well for the healthy functioning of a democratic state; if the communities of academics cited above could have been enticed back to their own countries by a swift reversal of policy as happened in 306 BC to the philosophers of Athens, the world would probably be a better place. But it is a fallacy to think that the stifling of academic freedom comes only from totalitarian regimes. Pressure can also come from a liberal society in a way that is less obvious than outright persecution, but still harmful to the intellectual growth of society. Academics of no particular political stance in British and American universities complain – usually off record – of not being allowed to speak freely in their own seminars for fear of breaking new rules of political correctness; the penalties include 'no-platforming' (when speakers are barred from public speaking events), and professional ostracism. Socrates, pilloried for his provocative views, seems oddly familiar today. If he showed us anything, it is that freedom of speech is one of the most powerful – and feared – elements of democratic society. There is a fundamental need to protect it, even when it transgresses the standards of what we happen to deem politically correct at any particular time.

From Direct to Representative Democracy

We as modern constituents vote for representatives who then vote on our behalf on big decisions. Referendums, though they seem to be getting more common, are not our primary method for expressing 'the will of the people', and this is the first major difference between our indirect democracy and ancient direct democracy. But another crucial difference is the deliberative nature of Athenian democracy, the opportunity for debate and input from everyone (not just politicians) on proposals before they are put to public vote. This is something that is sorely missing today, although it is making something of a comeback, as we shall explore later. The direct and deliberative elements of Athenian democracy were essentially due to the fact that, as a tiny state of around 50,000 citizens, it had the ability to truly put power in the hands of the people on an almost weekly basis; today, we choose intermediaries to represent us primarily because the size of our societies simply does not allow for constant direct input from everyone.

The nature of modern elective democracy has been much debated, particularly the loyalties of an elected Member of Parliament (or Congress, or any equivalent). Should these representatives be predominantly loyal to the interests of the constituents who chose them, or to the parliament as a whole – the collective will of the nation, as it were?

In 1774, Edmund Burke, Member of Parliament for Bristol, England, gave his seminal definition of the role of a Member of the British Parliament. Burke was highly sceptical of democracy working at all, except in very small states like ancient Athens. But since he found himself in power, he tried to define what he thought his duties were. His famous 'Speech to the Electors of Bristol at the Conclusion of the Poll' contained the following argument:

> *Parliament is not a congress of ambassadors from different and hostile interests; which interests each must maintain, as an agent and advocate, against other agents and advocates; but parliament is a deliberative assembly of one nation, with one interest, that of the whole; where, not local purposes, not local prejudices, ought to guide, but the general good, resulting from the general reason of the whole. You choose a member indeed; but when you have chosen him, he is not member of Bristol, but he is a member of parliament. If the local constituent should have an interest, or should form a hasty opinion, evidently opposite to the real good of*

*the rest of the community, the member for that place ought to be as
far, as any other, from any endeavour to give it effect.*[13]

But is a modern parliament really 'a deliberative assembly
of one nation'? The recent trials and tribulations of Brexit,
for example, would suggest that, if it is, the deliberation of
our elected representatives does not get us anywhere – partly
because they are confused about what they owe their constituents, their party or their own conscience when it comes to
making a decision as momentous as how to leave the European Union. They are concerned about getting it wrong in the
unforgiving glare of public scrutiny, or just straightforwardly
self-interested and trying to calculate which stance will play out
best for them in the long run. Indirect democracy muddies the
waters. If the British people themselves had some responsibility
in formulating a plan, it is possible (though not certain) that
they would not have voted to leave in the first place, because
with lack of responsibility comes cavalier decision-making.
Even more likely, they would not have experienced such a
conflict of interests in moving forward, because party politics
would not have got in the way of making a practicable plan
– though that is not to say that the wisdom of the crowd is
infallible, as we will discuss later.

One of the major episodes of Athenian democracy was the
Mytilenian Debate in 427 BC, during which the Assembly
argued about whether or not to vote again on a decision
already taken (explored in detail in Lesson Three of this book).

According to Thucydides, a speaker called Diodotus argued that citizens should be guided by orators like himself. Athenian orators were emphatically not the ancient equivalent of modern political representatives, but in this particular speech, a certain resemblance to the modern politician–citizen relationship can be seen. Essentially, Diodotus is saying, 'Let me guide you, but do not blame me for your collective errors of judgement' – a frustrating sentiment all too familiar to modern voters.

> *But it is right to expect we who discuss matters of the greatest importance ought to take a longer view than you who just look at the issues briefly, especially since we are held accountable for giving our advice, but you are not held accountable for listening to it. For if the man who gave advice and the man who took it suffered equally, you would consider things more moderately. But as it is, whenever some passion leads you to disaster, you only punish the judgement of your adviser and not your own judgement, even if many share responsibility for the error.*[14]

Our premise in this book is that enough meaningful parallels between ancient and modern democracy exist to illuminate what we can and should do better. The five lessons that follow are a kind of summons to the modern Pnyx for immediate deliberation – and top of the agenda is the question of how to inspire modern citizens with the same sense of urgency and political responsibility that Athenian citizens felt in the fifth century BC.

A MASTERCLASS IN DEMOCRACY FROM ANCIENT ATHENS

Lesson One:
Don't Be an *Idiotes*

Decree from the deme of Aixone in Attica honouring
local *choregoi* (theatre producers/sponsors), with relief
showing the god Dionysos, protector of theatre, attended by
satyr and theatrical masks carved above the scene.
(Epigraphical Museum, Athens)

No man is an island.

JOHN DONNE

The ancient Greek word *idiotes* – 'private citizen' – had the connotation of someone who was isolated from public affairs and ignorant. Athenian citizens were expected to engage in the public sphere, to listen, discuss freely and vote in an informed way – there were even specific words which encapsulated this, like *isegoria*, the equal right to speak in public, and *parresia*, the courage to express yourself freely.

The Athenian insistence on private citizens taking part in the public realm was not normal among the city states of ancient Greece. Pericles, in his great eulogy of Athens in 431 BC, boasted that: 'For we are unique in that we consider the man who takes no part in public affairs not to be apolitical, but useless.'[1] The Athenians were proud of their reputation for public engagement; in Euripides' play *Hippolytus* the tormented Phaedra expresses her dying wish as a mother: 'I want my sons to live as free men in this glorious city of Athens, flourishing because they can speak their minds [*parresia*].'[2] Her words are echoed by another great female advocate of free speech, the twentieth-century fashion designer Coco Chanel: 'The most courageous act is still to think for yourself. Aloud.'

When thousands of citizens gathered at an Assembly meeting on the Pnyx, the speaker of the house would stand up and shout: 'WHO WISHES TO SPEAK?' and anyone could approach the orator's platform and do so. The shortened phrase *ho boulomenos* in Greek – 'whoever wishes' – would be used in many political contexts; *ho boulomenos* was the citizen who would take the initiative of proposing a decree, for example, or who initiated a public prosecution, or who spoke up in a debate. In response, the crowd could (and often did) insert itself into the debate by making a collective *thorubos*, or clamour. We don't know to what extent the same opinionated people hogged the orator's platform – a trained orator or an elected general will have certainly spoken more than the average Joe, steadily building his reputation in the public eye much as popular commentators on Twitter grow and sustain their followers. However, lone voices from the Athenian crowd counted in a way we struggle to comprehend today, and the interaction between *ho boulomenos* and the crowd was the ultimate proof of open public engagement.

Today, when you stand in front of the orator's platform on the Pnyx, where the Assembly gathered to vote, you see the Acropolis to your right, and stretching ahead, a cityscape that was once fields of cultivated land. In the fifth century, the Pnyx had been arranged the other way, facing the sea to symbolize Athens' strength in its navy and openness to the world. The oligarchs who seized power after Athens' defeat at the hands of Sparta at the end of the fifth century, however, disapproved of this symbolism, and rearranged the Pnyx so that it was facing inland – literally inward-facing. According to the second-century AD Greek biographer Plutarch, they 'believed that Athens' naval empire had proved to be the mother of democracy and that an oligarchy was more easily accepted by men who tilled the soil'.[3] Today, too, the populations of coastal towns tend to hold more open-minded, liberal views than the conservative populations of the interior, such as the predominantly Democrat-supporting coastlines of the US, and the more secular communities of Turkey's coast.

As a response to the insecurity suffered after Athens' defeat and the loss of its empire, its democracy became less radical and more bureaucratic in the fourth century BC – it also ushered in an era of "experts". There was less confidence in the wisdom of the *demos*, and the Athenians adopted a defensive 'play it safe' system of government whereby power rested more in the hands of men deemed capable of taking charge than in the *demos* itself. The loss of empire also meant that funds dried up, and one major consequence was that the state became more dependent on private wealth. In the fourth century BC, the spectacular rise of Philip and his son Alexander the Great in Macedon increased the strain in Athenian democracy. Systems of public administration were modernized and reformed to become more efficient (hence, for example, the use of the *kleroterion*), and money began to be redirected to military operations as Athens felt Philip's shadow looming.

The great orator Demosthenes was among those who articulated the general uneasiness in Athenian society at the time. The 336 BC law against tyranny (the *stele* illustrated by the image of a personified Demokratia crowning Demos the old man) was passed shortly after the victory of Philip at Chaeroneia, north of Athens. Demosthenes helped Athenian democrats realize that the domination of Philip would be fatal to democracy –

as indeed it proved to be. Ironically, it was at this very time that the cult of worshipping Demokratia as a goddess became prominent in Athens, as if the Athenians were trying to exorcize the doomed fate of democracy that was soon to come – or appeal to a divine power to save their all-too-mortal system of government.

Like the old man in the famous *stele* image, Demosthenes was crowned in recognition of his role in protecting Athenian democracy, despite his political opponents' objections. He repeatedly urged the Athenians to save themselves before it was too late. His speech 'On the Crown' gives an account of how the Athenian assembly responded when news arrived that nearby Elatea had fallen to Philip in 339 BC. As he tells it, an emergency assembly was held at dawn to decide whether to resist or surrender:

At daybreak the next day, the presidents summoned the Council to the Council House, and the citizens flocked to the place of assembly. Before the Council could introduce the business and prepare the agenda, the whole body of citizens had taken their places on the hill [the Pnyx].

The Council arrived, the presiding Councillors formally reported the intelligence they had received, and the courier was introduced. As soon as he had told his tale, the marshal put the question:

'Who wishes to speak?'

No one came forward. The marshal repeated his question again and again, but still no one rose to speak, although all the

commanders were there, and all the orators, and although the
country with her civic voice was calling for the man who should
speak for her salvation; for we may justly regard the voice which
the crier raises as the laws direct, as the civic voice of our country.[4]

Sometimes, even if the civic spirit is there, in pressurized situations collective decision-making can end in paralysis.

Within a small state, it is painfully obvious that democracy relies on an informed and engaged electorate to function properly, a principle that sometimes gets lost in the noise of a democracy of millions. But we need this as much as the Athenians did. Voter turnout has been falling worldwide since the 1980s, mostly in Western democracies. The worst-case scenario of an unengaged electorate is no one voting at all, which means democracy would cease to function – but there are more insidious dangers in retreating from the public to the private sphere. Voting out of a sense of disinterested duty – literal box-ticking – fulfils only the mechanical function of democracy, not its essence; we need to feel invested as citizens for it to work properly.

A Three Musketeers spirit of 'all for one and one for all' seems outdated today. It is a sentiment most obviously required in a state of emergency, which is traditionally war, but increasingly natural or constitutional disasters, like Brexit. In 349 BC, as Philip of Macedon began to show signs of overcoming all the city states of Greece, Demosthenes made a last-ditch attempt to convince the Athenian public of the danger threatening them, urging every citizen to play their part in a speech that has a certain flavour of Henry V's 'band of brothers': 'Make up your minds; rouse your spirits; put your heart into the war, now or never; you should pay your contributions cheerfully; serve in person; leave nothing to chance. You have no longer the shadow of an excuse for not wanting to do what needs to be done.'[5]

It's a message that echoes through the centuries, still familiar from the posters put up across Britain during the First World War, in particular of Lord Kitchener, the Secretary of State for War, pointing a finger alongside the stern message: 'Your country needs you!' While this was a targeted request to British men to sign up (unsuccessful, hence the introduction of conscription in 1916), Demosthenes was making a more general plea for public engagement, to raise both morale and practical help – like contributing funds for the war effort. He expresses a sentiment that is in fact closer to President Kennedy's request in his inauguration address in 1961, in which he outlined America's role as a freedom-protecting, democratic superpower at a critical juncture in the Cold War: 'Ask not what your country can do for you – ask what you can do for your country.'

This type of patriotic exhortation can, in the wrong context, have sinister connotations. It is often used by totalitarian states pushing the dangerous narrative that citizens exist primarily to serve the state; just a decade before JFK's address, Senator McCarthy explicitly encouraged the American public to monitor their neighbours for Communist sympathies, a type of surveillance Westerners have tended to associate, ironically, with states like the Soviet Union.

One of the aims of democracy is that, in ideal circumstances, citizens are left to their own devices. There is a fine line between being a public-spirited citizen and being a busybody. Pericles first outlined the double-faceted, private−public nature of democracy in his famous Funeral Oration, arguing that democracy affords citizens not only the freedom to participate in the public (*demosion* or *koinon*) sphere, but also the freedom to live as they please in the private (*idion*) sphere, free from interference or even (importantly) the disapproval of their peers – the 'live and let live' attitude beloved by libertarians today, and threatened by the much-deplored nanny state.

There is an important distinction between types of freedom in a democracy that is often ignored. The freedom *to* (engage in government, enjoy certain privileges), as opposed to freedom *from* (outside interference) is a problem that has latterly been under the spotlight in the debate over Britain's sovereignty in recent years. Many people who voted for Brexit did so because they thought they were 'taking back control' of their country, as Britain would be free to ignore EU laws. In reality, Britain's freedom to interact economically, culturally and socially with the world will, in many cases, be curtailed by Brexit. The most compelling instance of this is that British citizens will most likely lose their freedom of movement – their ability to travel, work and live in the European Union. There is little glory to be had in cutting a nation off, alone and proud on a tiny island, as the Melians discovered at the hands of the Athenians in 416 BC (see Lesson Three).

Twitter: The Modern Agora

The central Agora of Athens was the physical space where the private and public spheres met. It was where people gathered before voting on the Pnyx, where they conducted private business deals, attended trials, listened to official announcements and gossiped. In the remains of the Agora today you can see the monument of the Eponymous Heroes of Athens, where bronze statues of ten mythical heroes, after which each Athenian tribe was named, stood above huge wooden boards bearing public notices – conscription lists, voting agendas, upcoming lawsuits, lists of public honours. The monument would have been the busiest part of the Agora, serving as a meeting spot for tribe members who would gather under the statue of their eponymous hero to socialize and read the news.

Twitter is the modern equivalent of the agora: a space where people exchange views (and insults) as private citizens (named or anonymous), as public figures (presidents and prime ministers are increasingly addicted), or both, with increasing overlap. Government ministries troll each other via their official accounts, companies advertise, newspapers encourage debate on the breaking news they post online and journalists source eyewitness accounts of varying validity from across the globe.

There are plenty of good aspects of Twitter, and millions of people are better informed because of their daily engagement – clearly, it fulfils some public need for discussion. Ten minutes trawling the site can teach you a lot, and it can also expose you to a lot of vitriol. That's the important difference between the ancient agora and Twitter – the latter is not a physical space. There is a disconnection from reality which encourages 'those dirty looks which cause offence' as described by Pericles, as well as reckless or deliberate sharing of misinformation. In this virtual arena there is woefully little accountability, especially for hate speech (and for the excessive accountability of Athenian democratic institutions, see Lesson Two). The quality of much of the engagement on Twitter in fact brings to mind 1930s and 1940s Fascism; this extract from Max Horkheimer and Theodor W. Adorno's 1944 book *Dialectic of Enlightenment* could be a haunting description of today's Twitter trolls:

> *Individuals can no longer talk to each other and know it: they therefore . . . ensure that there is no proper conversation and at the same time no silence. On a wider scale, the same is true: it is not possible to have a conversation with a Fascist. If anyone else speaks, the Fascist considers his intervention a brazen interruption. He is not accessible to reason, because for him reason lies in the other person's agreement with his own ideas.*[6]

Fascism in any era is characterized by the inability to listen to others, and we currently seem to be suffering a double whammy of an excess of Periclean 'dirty looks', and a lack of meaningful public engagement. While voter turnout has been falling, forums like Twitter arguably rob us of the impetus to engage meaningfully in politics by providing a false outlet for our frustrations – we shout madly into the void, and half expect that to yield results. The complexity of the confusing and depressing news cycle of recent years has meant that while some have been spurred on by the absurd drama of it to march in protests and sign online petitions, others have mentally 'checked out' and retreated to private spaces. The latter is the death knell of civic engagement and, ultimately, of democracy.

The Glue of Democracy

Imagine there were massive open-air screenings of Netflix premieres held on public holidays which everyone attended, from Bill Gates all the way down the income brackets of society. Bill Gates, or someone else in the top 1 per cent income bracket, would pay for the entire thing; those in the lowest income brackets would be compensated for their time so that they could miss work to attend, and everyone would sit and watch and comment on the quality of the entertainment together.

In Athens there was no gradation of taxes as we have today – only a supertax on the super-rich for the benefit of poorer members of society, which came in the guise of an expensive public responsibility known as a liturgy. In the fourth century

BC, all citizens were paid to attend the public votes which took place at the Assembly forty times a year, with a payment known as *misthos* (a word still used in modern Greek). There is great debate among scholars about why the Athenians introduced the voting *misthos* – whether enthusiasm for participating in democracy had begun to wane and some kind of monetary incentive was needed; or whether this was a progressive step to enfranchise the poor, who could otherwise not afford to miss work; or, more cynically, whether it was simply a ploy by certain demagogues to gain popularity (a charge thrown at Pericles in the fifth century BC when he introduced pay for jury service). Critics of Greece's far-left Syriza party, who held power in the wake of the 2008 economic crisis, made the same complaint about their habit of handing out a variety of *epidomata* (social dividend) payments to low-waged Greeks to maintain popularity.

Back to the Netflix screenings: Athenian citizens classed as impoverished were given money so that they could attend the theatrical festivals that happened several times a year – a payment known as the *theorikon*. According to Plutarch, the Athenian orator Demades hailed the *theorikon* as 'the glue of democracy' because it ensured that people across the social spectrum encountered each other on a regular basis – the wealthy patrons of the arts who were required by law to personally fund and manage the choruses of enormously expensive theatre festivals, the musicians and actors involved in the productions, and ordinary punters who attended them because they had been paid to have a day off work to indulge in cultural edification. A special rule prohibited moneylenders from approaching their clients in the crowd for unpaid loans on festival days, so that everyone could genuinely enjoy themselves. Most importantly, the festivals encouraged private citizens to step away from their *idiotes* personas to engage in public life in a context other than voting. A modern state paying citizens in the lowest income bracket to attend a cultural event would be a truly radical – but possibly transformative – development in today's democracy.

Demosthenes was a famous enemy of Demades, and the two did not see eye to eye on public expenditure – if Demades was the culture vulture, Demosthenes was the military hawk. In 349 BC, when Philip of Macedon was carrying out campaigns in the north of Greece, Demosthenes chided the Athenians for wasting money on needless public entertainment while disaster threatened. He did not himself suggest redirecting the funds reserved for theatre festivals to the military fund, because that would have been illegal (merely suggesting this was in fact punishable by the death penalty, so sacred was the democratic glue of the theatrical fund). Instead, he proposed a war tax, which was duly implemented. It was not, however, enough to stop the invasion of Philip and the ultimate fall of democracy.

With regard to the supply of money, you have money, men of Athens, you have more than anyone else has for military purposes. But you appropriate it yourselves, in the way you want. Now if you will spend it on the campaign, you have no need of a further supply; if not, you have — or rather, you have no supply at all. 'What!' someone will cry, 'do you actually move to use this money for military purposes?' No! for Zeus' sake, I do not. Only it is my opinion that we must provide soldiers and that there must be one uniform system of pay in return for service. Your opinion, however, is that you should, without any trouble, just appropriate the money for your festivals. Then the only alternative is a war tax, heavy or light, as circumstances demand. Only money we must have, and without money nothing can be done that ought to be done.[7]

Tax straddles the private and public lives of citizens and forces us to tackle the question of how to spend individuals' money for the common good – and indeed what 'the common good' actually amounts to. Just like today, running the institutions of Athenian democracy was expensive. During the fifth century BC, public funds came from taxing overseas allies (who became effectively subjects), a source of income which dried up after the fall of the Athenian empire in 403 BC. In the fourth century BC, the absence of overseas taxes was made up for by much stricter and more efficient government, and by the existing system of taxes, benefits and financial incentives that had been set up in the fifth century BC. Liturgies were crucial, not just for funds, but because they brought down the super-rich by several pegs.

Community Service for the Super-Rich

The two major responsibilities imposed on the super-wealthy in ancient Athens were to produce choruses for the theatrical festivals (the role of *choregos*), and to personally captain and equip warships (*trierarchos*) – an even more demanding job. There was, moreover, an important extra democratic benefit that we do not have in our modern tax system. The liturgies involved both financial and non-financial duties, so the wealthy individual in question could not get away with just writing a big cheque, but had to engage personally with the job in a dizzying array of logistical, creative and mundane roles – this was no empty virtue-signalling.

If we take the case of a producer of a chorus for the theatrical performances (*choregos*), he was responsible for the following: recruiting the chorus, hiring an appropriate chorus trainer, and when the chorus involved music he also had to find a virtuoso flute-player. He had to feed the chorus, source and pay for their costumes, and find a place for them to rehearse. The personal involvement of the *choregos* and in fact all the liturgists in their duties meant that the rich individuals who might tend to detach themselves from the rest of society instead remained connected and loyal to the collective *demos* – and the effect was two-way.

Super-wealthy citizens generally accepted these responsibilities because they were legally required to do so, and because they came with huge honour and public gratitude (*charis*)

– comparable to the social standing of major philanthropic business dynasties like the Rockefeller or Niarchos families in New York and Athens today (it must be noted that the liturgy was emphatically a tax rather than an optional gift). Super-wealthy citizens' past liturgical duties were often used as mitigating factors in court cases; here is an example from the orator Lysias concerning the family of the general Nicias (who features in Lesson Three):

> *They were conscious of the honour in which the whole family were held by the city . . . and how they had made many large contributions to your funds, and had most nobly performed their public services involving vast expenditures; how they had never once evaded any of the other duties enjoined on them by the city, but had eagerly discharged all public services.* [8]

Likewise, Alcibiades, a charismatic general with rock star status (and ex-pupil of Socrates), boasted of his history of liturgies to prove that he deserved to lead the invasion of Sicily in 415 BC:

> *And again, any brilliance I display in the city by providing choruses or otherwise is naturally going to cause envy among my fellow citizens, but among the foreigners it will appear a sign of strength. This is not useless folly, when a man at his own private expense benefits not only himself but also his city.* [9]

However, sometimes the chosen millionaires refused to take on the responsibility, arguing that another millionaire was in fact in a better position to pay, and an undignified squabble broke out between them. They would then be ordered to swap their respective assets – a threat that usually led to agreement.

A modern democratic state ordering the super-wealthy to swap their assets if they refuse to pay for public works is a tantalizing idea, if unlikely in the arena of global capitalism. What is more viable is the idea of creating a system that actually engages wealthy people with the rest of society, as the liturgies did. Philanthropy can be a great thing, but also allows the philanthropist to function on a different plane to those she or he benefits, more like an ATM than a participant. It also affords a degree of moral credibility that might be at odds with the donor's business ventures.

In 2019, the Sackler family, owners of the American company Purdue Pharma, were ordered to pay $270 million in a settlement to the state of Oklahoma for their instigation of the opioid crisis as creators of the drug OxyContin – just one of hundreds of lawsuits the family have faced across America. The Sackler family have been major philanthropists, donating to universities and museums across the world, but their money has become toxic. If they had given their money in a form that necessitated personal involvement – for example, not merely donating to a museum but both paying the costs of and running a chain of hospitals or homeless shelters that cared for drug addicts – they would have been confronted by the consequences of their products, and perhaps America's crippling opioid crisis could have been reined in at an earlier stage.

Having a Go in Downing Street

The Athenian system of sortition and rotation meant that a huge proportion of the citizen population would have served in the Council of Five Hundred at some point – comparable to millions of British citizens taking turns preparing policy in Downing Street – as well as the 700 other public offices that were selected by lot every year. The annual members of the Council had to understand in depth every single agenda item of the Assembly to make preliminary decisions; in ten years there would be approximately 5,000 in this position, and in a generation (thirty years), there would be around 15,000 citizens – nearly half the electorate – with first-hand experience of creating laws from scratch. While serving on the Council, they would have taken it in turns, tribe by tribe, to serve on an executive committee called the *prytaneis* for thirty-five days before being replaced by the next tribe, so that by the end of the year all members of the Council of Five Hundred would have served as *prytaneis*. During those thirty-five days they lived in a round hut called the Tholos, the *prytaneis* headquarters equivalent to 10 Downing Street; the foundation stones of the Tholos are just about visible in the Agora today, as are scanty remains of the building that housed the Council of Five Hundred.

Obviously, we cannot achieve the same proportion of citizen involvement in policy-making with the size of our electorates today – half of the electorate of the United Kingdom, for example, would be tens of millions of ordinary citizens passing through the door of Number 10 over the course of thirty years, rather than tens of thousands. But we can still engage the electorate far more than we do now, via random selection on a smaller scale. Citizen assemblies are already gathering pace in parts of the world – something we will come to in the last section of this book.

Democracy is primarily about equality: affording everyone an equal voice, equal protection and equal opportunity. The principle of 'the wisdom of the crowd', however, is different – it is the argument that the crowd, or *demos*, actually knows best, ethics aside. It is a principle that features in hard-nosed global markets today, and in information crowdsourcing endeavours like Wikipedia. In ancient times the wisdom of the crowd was a highly controversial idea. It still has its detractors today, in an age when the crowd is given considerably less credence, in a political context, than it was two and a half millennia ago.

Crowds vs. Experts

How do we decide, collectively, whether abortion should be legal? Or whether our country should withdraw from an international union? Should we trust in each other, or in 'experts' – whoever they are? And how do we establish what the *demos* wants – by giving everyone a one-off vote, or by getting a cross-section of society to thrash out all the issues, or both?

The ancient Athenians had both direct democracy – our equivalent of a referendum – and deliberative democracy – the relatively uncommon modern practice of a citizens' assembly. The whole system was geared up to tap the wisdom of the crowd, even though prominent critics, like the father of Western philosophy, disapproved of election by lot. According to his pupil Xenophon, Socrates thought the wisdom of experts was what was needed in government, just as it is in any other field. Why would you employ a random person as a naval pilot, for example, if you need a good navigator? 'Nobody would employ a candidate chosen by lot as a naval pilot or a carpenter or a flute player, nor any other craftsman for work in which mistakes are far less disastrous than mistakes in matters related to the state.'[10]

Plato, another of Socrates' pupils, is more famous for suggesting that only the wisest should rule the *demos*. His work *The Republic* imagines a utopian city called Kalipolis ('Beautiful City') which would work in real life 'if philosophers become kings . . . or if those now called kings . . . genuinely and adequately philosophize'. Plato's idea of a 'philosopher king' was, according to the twentieth-century philosopher Karl Popper, a dangerous precursor to the modern ideology of totalitarianism – the complete subservience of a state to an all-knowing leader or regime, something utterly incompatible with democracy.[11]

85

The 'Old Oligarch' is the name given by early twentieth-century Anglo-American classicists to an anonymous, pro-Spartan Athenian who may or may not have been Xenophon, writing a 'Constitution of the Athenians' in the fifth century BC. He unapologetically criticizes the undue respect given to 'worthless' (i.e. ordinary) men at the expense of the 'worthy' (i.e. wealthy and educated) men in a democratic society:

> *I do not approve of the fact that [the Athenians] have chosen to have this type of constitution for the following reason, that in making their choice they have chosen that the worthless men should do better than the worthy . . . within the demos there is the greatest ignorance, indiscipline and worthlessness. For poverty tends to lead them into shameful behaviour, and in the case of some people their lack of education and their ignorance is the result of their lack of money.*[12]

The Old Oligarch (to a British ear, this has irresistible echoes of 'Old Etonian') argues that establishing a democracy is misguided because it comes at the expense of good government. He implicitly questions the notion of a common good and suggests that 'valuable' men might not be particularly interested in acting in the interests of the 'worthless', and vice versa. In the end, he concludes that democracy achieves the most desirable results for the 'worthless' man, which ensures its popularity with the masses.

Any worthless person who wishes can stand up in the assembly and procure what is good for himself and those like him. Someone might say, 'How could such a person recognize what is good for himself and the demos?' But the Athenians know that this man's ignorance and worthlessness and good will are more advantageous to them than are the excellence and wisdom and ill will of the valuable man.[13]

Modern commentators are usually less rude about 'the ordinary man', but the nineteenth-century Scottish journalist Charles Mackay summed up a common feeling in his 1841 book *Extraordinary Popular Delusions and the Madness of Crowds*. 'Men, it has been well said, think in herds. It will be seen that they go mad in herds, while they only recover their sense slowly, and one by one.'[14]

This was best illustrated in ancient Greece in 406 BC, when the Athenians fought the Spartans at the naval battle of Arginusae. The Athenians won, but their generals failed to collect their dead from the sea because of a storm. When the generals returned to Athens there was an outcry, and oligarchic sympathizers took advantage of the anger and grief of the crowd to demand an illegal group trial of the generals. When some members of the presiding council declared that they would not back the motion, the oligarchic sympathizers bribed a man called Callixenus to put forward the same charge against them. Xenophon tells us that Socrates, who happened to be serving on the presiding committee at this trial, was the sole voice to speak out against 'the madness of herds', but he was ignored and indeed blamed for his interference: 'The majority of the crowd cried out that it would be monstrous if the people were to be prevented from doing whatever they wished'[15] – a striking manifestation of the tyranny of the majority, a concept coined by the French political theorist Alex de Tocqueville. In the event, the crowd had their way, and the generals were all illegally executed.

Two generations removed from Socrates, his indirect pupil Aristotle was a lonely voice among ancient philosophers in his (qualified) support for democracy, specifically for the idea that the collective is a better judge than the single expert, an idea that also underpinned the invention of a jury to decide a man's innocence or guilt.

It is possible that the many, though not individually men of excellence, yet when they come together may be better, not individually but collectively, than the few who are so, just as a feast to which many contribute is better than a dinner provided out of a single purse. For each individual among the many has a share of excellence and practical wisdom, and when they meet together, just as they become in a manner one man, who has many feet, and hands, and senses, so too with regard to their character and thought. Hence the many are better judges than a single man of music and poetry; for some understand one part, and some another, and among them, they understand the whole.[16]

In the twenty-first century, the wisdom of the crowd is harnessed much more effectively in capitalist ventures than in flawed democratic states – partly because actual money is at stake. Enterprises like Lego, for example, are companies which have profited enormously from legions of loyal über-fans who want to freely contribute ideas to a brand to which they are devoted. Formed in 1949, and named 'the world's most powerful brand' by the independent consultancy Brand Finance in 2015,[17] Lego has an almost unparalleled community of fans, from which it receives around 20,000 ideas for new products every year.[18]

Although it is considered primarily a company that makes products for children, the adult division of Lego is far more profitable, largely because of the obsessiveness of adult fans – it made perfect commercial sense to build what these big-spending customers ask for. Lego Ideas is the company's official online fan community (there are hundreds of unofficial fan sites), and it is run as a virtual democracy – the serious version of Legoland. Contests are run for new product ideas, and if any entry gets at least 10,000 votes from other users of the site, the in-house designers review with a view to making it. The company rather smugly reports an overall 'customer satisfaction rate' of 95–97 per cent,[19] which is unsurprising – if customers feel important, they feel happy.

It seems unlikely that any democratic country in the world today would truthfully report a 95–97 per cent satisfaction rate among its citizens – and there is indeed something distasteful about envisaging democracy as a user experience. Perhaps the ultimate example of disinterested deliberative democracy is Wikipedia, the free online encyclopaedia, which is better than any professionally produced encyclopaedia in the world, its entries crowdsourced and surprisingly well policed and the whole enterprise funded by those who use it. In a sense, it encapsulates the rather unexpected analogy of the dinner party in Aristotle's appraisal of the wisdom of the crowd – 'a feast to which many contribute is better than a dinner provided out of a single purse'.

Aristotle was a philosopher, not a politician – he was analytical rather than opportunistic. But the ability to evoke the wisdom of the crowd was a classic tool of flattery employed by demagogues like Cleon, who was a prominent figure in Athenian democracy during the latter half of the fifth century BC. He features in Thucydides' account of the Mytilenian Debate in 427 BC (see Lesson Three), where he argues – somewhat patronizingly – that the 'intellectually naive' make the best citizens because they are not always trying to prove their cleverness.

The most frightening thing of all is that we will not stand fast over anything we have decided, and that we will not recognize that a city is stronger by following worse but steadfast laws than having good laws that have no authority, and that ignorance with self-control is more advantageous than cleverness with intemperance, and that on the whole men of lower rank better run cities than those of greater intellect. For these latter types want to appear wiser than the laws and always try to get their way in every discussion about ordinary matters, because they cannot show their judgement in more important matters, and for this reason too often bring ruin to their cities. But the other type, those that are not so confident in their own intelligence, think it right to be less learned than the laws and less capable at finding flaws in the arguments of a good speaker, and being impartial judges rather than competitors they generally conduct affairs successfully. This is what we ought to do as well, and not get carried off by cleverness and contests of intellect and advise this assembly against its own judgement.[20]

This idea that intelligent individuals are a dangerous presence among voters has been spouted in recent years by right-wing politicians like Donald Trump and Michael Gove, who tend to refer to academics, economists and scientists whose opinions they disagree with as 'experts'. Two weeks before the Brexit referendum in June 2016, Michael Gove, one of the figureheads of the Vote Leave campaign, declared on national television that 'people in this country have had enough of experts' – referring to the predictions made by economists that leaving the EU would seriously damage the UK's economy. The result of the referendum of course proved Gove right in one sense – the *demos* does not like being told it is wrong (President Trump is also a champion denouncer of experts, and his election was also validation that this is a winning line).

Whether Oxford-educated Gove was right on a moral level

to claim to speak for the common man and dismiss 'the experts' advising the country is another question. There is an obvious irony in him apparently speaking for the common man as he scorns the advice of economists, given his Oxford degree; Trump, with his enormous inherited wealth and golden elevators, is even more risible as a 'common man' when he claims to understand his hard-working voter base. President Erdoğan of Turkey, who at least did grow up in a poor area of Istanbul, worked as a bus driver before entering politics and refers to his supporters as 'my brothers', is a figure with whom his supporters can genuinely identify. Erdoğan is king of the expert-haters – he especially hates the IMF, Western analysts or academics of any background, but particularly Turkish – and his own 'man of the people' background somehow gives this stance weight in the eyes of his voters. However, in general it matters little whether a populist is genuinely from an ordinary background or not; the arguments still work.

Thomas Jefferson, one of the founding fathers of the United States of America, while undoubtedly held in much greater esteem than Trump, was also firmly in the Cleon camp, almost replicating his argument that the 'intellectually naive' make better citizens because of, rather than despite, their lack of education. 'State a moral case to a ploughman and a professor. The former will decide it as well and often better than the latter because he has not been led astray by artificial rules.'

And talking of agricultural parables, one of the most famous experiments in testing the wisdom of the crowd is given to us by James Surowiecki at the beginning of his important book *The Wisdom of Crowds*.[21] He tells us the story of the scientist Sir Francis Galton, who was initially convinced that the crowd is *not* wise and set out to prove it. Galton attended a country fair in 1906, at which there was a competition which is still popular in various guises: Guess the Weight of the Ox. Eight hundred people competed, and after the entries had been collected and the closest guess rewarded, Galton asked the organizers for all the submitted entry slips (a few of which were illegible) and examined them. To his surprise, when he calculated the mean entry, it was 1,197lb, almost identical to the ox's real weight of 1,198lb – the collective wisdom of the crowd was spot on, with the guesses of the informed offsetting the guesses of the ill-informed, and the conservative offsetting the rash. It is ironic, of course, that Galton, a wise individual – even, perhaps, an 'expert' – was wrong about the crowd getting it wrong.

One of the most controversial elements of applying the wisdom of the crowd to a particular decision-making process is the question of whether the members of the crowd should confer, or make their decisions separately. For example, with the Galton experiment, if all the people who entered the 'Guess the Weight of the Ox' experiment had conferred with each other, their collective guess would undoubtedly have been skewed by opinionated and persuasive members of the crowd. Crucially, they did not confer as a group; what Galton realized was that the entries were the true reflection of what everyone really thought, and their average was almost spot on.

Arguably, the Athenian jury system, involving hundreds of people who voted via a secret ballot on the guilt or innocence of a defendant, was far superior to a modern jury of twelve who confer and are potentially subject to the persuasion of others – too bad that collecting hundreds of people for every trial would be an impossible task today.

James Surowiecki argues that, 'given enough information and the chance to talk things over with peers, ordinary people are more than capable of understanding complex issues and making meaningful choices about them'. That sounds reasonable, but it is not a given that an electorate composed of millions of people exposed to targeted propaganda more sophisticated than in any previous era have the freedom to do this. Random people can be expected to make a fair guess at the weight of an ox – they've seen oxen before, and they've guessed weights before. But making a fair guess at how an undefined withdrawal from an international body might work out – for example – is very different. Critics of referendums argue that trying to tap the wisdom of the crowd on a binary question is dangerous, because by its nature the question introduces polarized camps of opponents, and becomes a matter of 'which side do you belong to?' rather than 'what do you think is the right course of action?'

Rather than being open to debate, people dug their heels in on either side of the Brexit question in the run-up to the referendum, and have continued to do so. This polarization developed even though arguably the question posed on the ballot paper – to remain in or leave the European Union – was not as binary as it appeared to be, since the terms of leaving were never spelled out. If the Brexit referendum had allowed the public to say, 'we want to stay in the EU but only on these conditions' or 'we want to leave but only on these conditions', it might not have led to such a close and bitterly divisive result. The Athenian Assembly, rather than accepting a proposal of the Council of Five Hundred wholesale, or rejecting it out of hand, were allowed to suggest a modification to a proposal they overall supported, but had reservations about – a subsequent vote would be taken on the proposed amendment then and there. Unfortunately, granting that kind of agency to an electorate the size of Britain's would be hard to execute, and, for the moment at least, we are left with reductive, two-option referendums.

Rather than answering 'yes' or 'no' questions, the crowd possesses a wisdom better suited to establishing a mean, like the weight of the ox, or the price of something (the stock market is remarkably good in the short term at determining the correct value of a company). The crowd also positively enjoys answering open-ended questions – like deciding on a choice of name. Just three months before the Brexit referendum in 2016, an online poll called *#NameOurShip* was conducted in Britain to come up with a name for the lead ship of a research mission operated by the British Antarctic Survey. The team would be conducting research for the legendary naturalist and TV presenter Sir David Attenborough, universally acknowledged to be a national treasure. Perhaps because of the feeling of ownership that the British public has over Sir David, it was decided that they should be given a voice in the name of the flagship for his research.

The British people were given a voice, and they spoke: *Boaty McBoatface*, a name initially suggested as a joke on a radio show, but which became immensely popular and ended up winning the poll. In a grave miscarriage of democratic justice, however, *Boaty McBoatface* did not become the name of the lead research vessel on the expedition – instead, the Minister for Universities and Science, Jo Johnson, decided that it would be named *Sir David Attenborough*, which of course no one could be too cross about (although, in response, a petition was created to demand that Attenborough change his name to Boaty McBoatface). In a way, the Boaty McBoatface saga expressed the essence of British irreverent humour and disregard for po-faced authority – it was two fingers to the establishment, as, arguably, the Brexit vote came to be three months later.

The Whim of the Crowd

If governments are to resort to referendums, they have to work out how to use them responsibly. One particularly salutary lesson from history is Hitler granting himself the power to hold referendums, which he did to consolidate his regime in the early 1930s, most notably the 1934 referendum in which Germans effectively voted for their own dictator, approving the merging of the posts of president and chancellor to make him 'Führer'. In 1933, 95 per cent of voters had backed Hitler's proposal to leave the League of Nations, a resounding 'yes' to a question that sounds remarkably grandiose to modern ears: 'Do you approve, German man, and you, German woman, this policy of your national government, and are you willing to declare it as the expression of your own opinion and your own will and solemnly profess it?' Ever since the end of the Second World War in 1945, Germany has not held a national referendum.

A democracy like Britain, whose system is designed to entrust elected representatives to make decisions of policy, is particularly ill-suited to holding the odd, monumentally important decision to which the answer can only be one of two options. Switzerland, on the other hand, which has always been something of an outlier as a country by virtue of its almost aggressive neutrality and independence, is addicted to referendums both at local and national level. In 1848, it was the first country to introduce the referendum as a modern incarnation of the Athenian Assembly vote, and it has held four hundred in the last fifty years. The country is unusual not just in holding plebiscites to confirm or deny a government proposal, but in allowing individual citizens to challenge government decisions by proposing a referendum of their own – much like the 'who wishes to speak?' process on the Pnyx. The state website describes the referendum process as follows: 'When citizens disagree with the decision of Parliament and they gather 50,000 valid signatures within 100 days of the official publication of the act, or eight cantons submit a request, the act is submitted to a vote of the People (an optional referendum). The act only comes into force if it is accepted by the majority of the People.'[22] Unlike most countries, Switzerland's most important referendum results are not advisory but binding – the government has to do what the people say.

Some of the results of these referendums have been impressively public-spirited – the Swiss have voted to increase their own taxes and go without an extra week of paid holiday, for example. Arguably, their long history of heading to the polls several times a year has made them understand the nature of trade-offs and the public good – but this is not universally the case in places where direct democracy has been adopted. The state of California has been plagued by the excessive power enjoyed by its citizens – a combination of recalls, in which voters can get rid of elected officials in midterm if they fail to live up to expectations (this brings to mind the ancient Athenians' draconian punishment of unpopular politicians); referendums, in which they can reject new laws (like the Swiss); and initiatives, in which they write their own. In 2011, the state was effectively bankrupted because Californians voted not to raise taxes.

What happens when the majority takes a decision which suppresses the rights of a minority – for example, when direct democracy overrules the egalitarian system of values on which modern democracy is supposed to rest? In 2009, well before the European refugee crisis started, 57.5 per cent of the Swiss electorate voted to ban the building of minarets, a discriminatory measure that reflected, ostensibly, the distaste that the majority of Swiss people had for this feature of the landscape, but more realistically a rejection of the country's Muslim minority. It also took the country's male population two national referendums to decide to give women the vote. After 67 per cent of Swiss men rejected the idea in 1959, it was posed again in 1971, and this time won by nearly the same percentage (66 per cent). Even then, women did not have the vote on a local level in all cantons until 1991. In the über-traditional canton of Appenzel, instead of a secret ballot at a polling station, men simply gather in the central square and each pull a ceremonial bayonet from its sheath to indicate 'yes'. In 1990, most swords remained firmly sheathed in response to the question of whether to allow women the vote, so in 1991 the Federal Court intervened to overrule this. Even today, while men can still vote with their swords, women wield a much less exciting voting card.

Switzerland is the only country to have granted women the vote via a referendum – it is very likely that if other countries had used the same method, there would still be plenty of nominally democratic countries with a disenfranchised female population. Voters are often more hardcore conservatives than elected politicians, as Switzerland has proved several times. Five years after the 2009 minaret referendum, in 2014, the country voted to curb immigration by stopping the freedom of movement that had been a prerequisite of its access to the EU's single market; given the potential ramifications to the economy, the Swiss government took the extremely unusual step of disregarding the outcome of the referendum. Later that year, a group of Swiss students and activists started a liberal movement called Operation Libero, which has since been credited with pushing back against the right-wing nationalism of the past couple of decades, embodied in parties like the right-wing Swiss People's party (SVP).

Sometimes, even people keen on direct democracy can decide that enough is enough. In November 2018, Switzerland voted against a proposal to put its own laws above international laws, a move which would have seriously damaged the economy and the country's international standing. Sometimes, too much sovereignty can be a bad thing, and luckily the *demos* can be better than dictators at realizing this.

Deliberation Day

Even if the terms of Brexit had been decided in advance and clarified on the ballot paper, it was arguably irresponsible to pose a question of that magnitude without equipping voters to fully understand all its ramifications. What Britain needed was Deliberation Day, which sounds like a cerebral version of a Hollywood disaster movie, but is in fact an idea proposed by two political scientists, James Fishkin and Bruce Ackermann, as a radical new tool for American democracy.[23] Deliberation Day would be a public holiday which would take place two weeks before national elections, bringing voters together to talk in organized groups about the major issues at play. They would be paid $150 for this – much like the pay that was introduced in fourth-century Athens for attendance at the Assembly.

The idea of getting people to debate political issues in person is a great one, but payment in return for deliberating or voting is a controversial idea. Compensating less well-off citizens for their time is one thing, but a blanket cash reward for everyone is more problematic. Should citizens be financially motivated to perform one of the very few responsibilities that come with living in a democracy? Voting is not a service, and citizens are not employees of a democratic state, but arguably, as soon as you introduce a monetary incentive, you create that kind of relationship. If, however, it is only way to get disengaged citizens to vote, perhaps it is worth it – much like the attitude of parents who pay their children to finish homework. It is even more worth it to get people to really think about what they are voting for.

Abortion is probably one of the most emotional and divisive issues of our times; politicians often hesitate to nail their colours to the mast because they know their stance will automatically lose them votes from one side of the debate, especially in the most polarized 'liberal vs. conservative' Western countries. Perhaps this is why a decades-long impasse in Ireland was finally solved with the help of a citizens' assembly composed of one hundred random members of the public (selected via stratified sampling). Since a 1983 referendum introduced the eighth amendment to the Irish constitution, equating the rights of the unborn child to the rights of the mother, abortion had been in almost every case illegal; the passage of thirty years, however, had brought a growing demand for change from the public – yet not clearly enough expressed to get politicians to repeal the amendment.

The citizens' assembly began to deliberate the issue on weekends starting in October 2016, along with other polarizing issues like how to tackle (or indeed acknowledge) climate change. As in ancient Athens, these citizens plucked from their private lives for public service were compensated with a nominal fee for their time, but were not given salaries; they live-streamed their meetings on social media and invited comments and suggestions from the public, opening up the decision-making process rather than cutting it off from view. During their sessions, they were made to listen to speeches from activists on both sides of the debate, like Athenian voters on the Pnyx, as well as audio recordings of Irish women who had travelled abroad for abortions, and those who had not. There was also a facilitator on hand to ensure no one monopolized the conversation – averting the scenario of one persuasive individual directing the course of debate, and ensuring that everyone's questions were put to the table.

The conclusions of the citizens' assembly in April 2017 made global headlines: a majority of the participants (64 per cent) advised the government to allow Irish women unrestricted access to abortion. The referendum that took place the following year confirmed this among the wider public; two-thirds of the electorate voted to overturn the abortion ban, almost mirroring the majority of the citizens' assembly who had voted the same way. The result confirmed the move towards liberal values expressed in the 2015 referendum, in which Ireland became the first country in the world to legalize gay marriage by referendum, with an irrefutable majority of 62 per cent, which likewise took place after a citizens' assembly convened in 2013.

The success of the Irish citizens' assemblies encouraged British politicians, activists and academics to push for a similar assembly during the torturous stasis in the run-up to Britain's planned departure from the EU on 29 March 2019. As time ran out, the gap began to close for the potential assembly to achieve anything meaningful, even if it were approved by Parliament. Four months before the exit date of 29 March 2019, Neal Lawson, the chair of the pressure group Compass, proposed a citizens' assembly for Brexit in the following terms in an essay for Open Democracy:[24]

The remit for the Brexit Citizens Assembly would be to decide between no deal, a deal or a second referendum. The assembly would take a few months to deliberate and decide, meaning Article 50 would need to be temporarily delayed. And while Parliament cannot be bound by any external body, the moral and political pressure to abide by the decisions of the Assembly would be irresistibly strong. If Parliament cannot decide, then this is possibly the only way to start to reunite our fractured nation.

There was scepticism of his and others' endorsement of the citizens' assembly, which was understandable given the entrenched polarization of views and general despair evoked by

Brexit nearly three years in, and the fact that no such assembly had been conducted on this scale in the UK, let alone on a matter of such importance. Would this mysterious assembly be a real representation of the British public's views? Would it be legitimate, and fairly conducted? What if Parliament refused to accept its recommendations – would we then not be in even more of a mess than before?

Needless to say, no Brexit citizens' assembly took place, but it should have done. At the very least, Ackermann and Fishkin's vision of Deliberation Day would have been extremely helpful before the original Brexit referendum; a day to address important issues, to encounter opposing views in a civil environment (in both sense of the word), to break the addiction we all have to our echo chambers, whether in the real world or online. Even if the referendum result had been the same afterwards, it would have engendered a sense of collective responsibility which is missing in the fractured electorate of Britain today.

Lesson Two:
Stop the Demagogues

Ostraka (pot sherds), bearing the names of famous
Athenian politicians of the fifth century BC who risked exile:
Aristeides, Themistocles, Kimon and Pericles.
(Agora Museum, Athens)

What was in name a democracy was in fact the rule of the
principal man.

THUCYDIDES

We can all name a democracy that is in fact a government of the principal man. Donald Trump, Recep Tayyip Erdoğan, Narendra Modi and Jair Bolsonaro, among others, all came to power promising to represent the ordinary, hard-working voter ignored by the undefined 'elite' establishment. In doing so, they used techniques which have been in use since 508 BC – and even before democracy began, among the aristocrats who competed for power in ancient Athens.

'*Prostates tou demou*' ('the one who stands before the people' or 'protector of the people') was the term used in the late fifth century to refer to the leader of the citizen body of Athens, conveying the aura of guardianship that modern 'principal men' still love to channel. Although the words could be used in a positive sense, they also sounded the same alarm bells we hear today when our world leaders refer to themselves in similar terms – *prostates tou demou* was used with deeply negative connotations in both comic contexts (Aristophanes) and tragic (Euripides). Today's equivalent of a 'principal man' is often a populist (from the Latin *popularis* – someone who promotes a political agenda that is popular with the people), who also has a lot in common with the most hated of Athenian figures, the demagogue – a rabble-rouser who drags rather than leads the people.

President Erdoğan is probably the best modern example of the overlap between demagogue and populist – he has all the spluttery vehemence of Cleon, for example, with some of the flair for crowd-pleasing psychology employed by an orator like Pericles. However, modern 'strongmen' populists indulge in a level of self-aggrandizement that would have been laughed to scorn in ancient Athens, particularly about their personal physical prowess. To give a few brief examples: the sixty-eight-year-old Modi making repeated claims about his '56-inch chest'[25] (two inches short of Arnold Schwarzenegger's at the height of his body-building fame), seventy-two-year-old Trump insisting on his excellent genes[26] and the beauty of his hands,[27] the then sixty-year-old Erdoğan being allowed to score a hat-trick in a football game against other famous Turkish people,[28] and the number one macho superman, a middle-aged, bare-chested Putin astride a horse in the wilds of Russia.[29] Even the great Athenian generals who won victories against the Spartans would have been embarrassed to allude to their chests, bared or otherwise.

Populist techniques work. Pericles – the 'principal man' of Athens for around twenty-five years in the mid fifth century – emerges from most of the ancient sources as an impressive, eloquent democrat who used his charisma to persuade his audiences to do what he believed best for them. Thucydides' sympathetic portrait of his handling of angry Athenian crowds after a plague struck Athens at the beginning of the Peloponnesian War contains gems of political psychology which remain useful for populists today: 'Pericles attempted to stop the Athenians from being angry with him, and guided their thoughts away from their immediate sufferings. As a community he succeeded in convincing them: they stopped sending emissaries to Sparta, and concentrated their energy on the war.'[30] The suggestion that it was only via carefully deployed charm that Pericles could persuade the Athenian people to act in their own interests (by focusing on the war, in this case) is a possible defence for any populist, and one that is rightly treated with suspicion.

The relationship between a strongman populist and an electorate can be seen like that of a man who passionately persuades his girlfriend that he is the only man she can trust, he is the only one who loves her and understands her despite her faults – the electorate, in return, feels protected and grateful, and increasingly fearful of losing him. Like all manipulative relationships, it has the potential to completely fall apart when the victim wakes up to the deception, or simply loses patience, as the Athenian electorate did with Pericles – who, while at the most benign end of the populist spectrum, still played the game of courting his audience, and occasionally lost. 'The general ill-feeling against Pericles persisted, and was not satisfied until the Athenians had forced him to pay a fine,' Thucydides reports, which they did after forcing him to stand trial in around 430 BC, with 1,500 (or 1,501) jurors who found him guilty of embezzlement. 'However, not long afterwards, as is the way with crowds, they re-elected him as general and put all their affairs in his hands.' Generals have a way of making a comeback – take, for example, the current president of Nigeria, Muhammadu Buhari, a former military dictator with a history of imprisoning critics and waging a violent 'war against indiscipline' in the 1980s. In 2015, aged seventy-two, he won a general election on his fourth try by claiming to be a born-again democrat who had learned from his mistakes.

According to Plato, the ever-sceptical Socrates (who admittedly was not a fan of democracy in general) held the view that Pericles was nothing more than a demagogue who was reduced to introducing payment for public office to remain popular.

Are the Athenians said to have become better because of Pericles, or quite the contrary, to have been corrupted by him? What I hear is that Pericles has made the Athenians idle, cowardly, talkative, and avaricious, by starting the system of public pay . . . Pericles made the Athenians more savage than when he took them in hand, and that against himself, the last person he would have wished them to attack.[31]

Like the military generals-turned-dictators of the twentieth century, Pericles took advantage of a political climate in which generals enjoyed extra prestige and authority on the Pynx. Unlike a run-of-the-mill General Sisi or Pinochet heading a military junta, Pericles was not an autocrat; a more acceptable comparison is perhaps Mustafa Kemal Pasha, the great general who became 'Atatürk', the father of modern Turkey, in 1923. Like Pericles, Atatürk was the nation's beloved, the architect of democratic change. He built a new republic and a parliament out of the remains of an empire, but he loomed so large on the political scene that he had no viable challengers, a situation which is of course not ideal in any democracy. Barack Obama noted this phenomenon when he talked of Nelson Mandela's ascension to power at an event honouring his legacy in South Africa in 2018: 'Madiba [Mandela's clan name] reminds us that democracy is about more than just elections. When he was freed from prison, Madiba's popularity – well, you couldn't even measure it. He could have been president for life. Am I wrong? Who was going to run against him?'

Pericles was elected general repeatedly over two decades – including for fifteen years in a row – and proposed all his policies in the Assembly not as a random member of the crowd but as someone who already had huge political clout; later, in fourth-century Athens, orators and generals worked in pairs, one doing the speaking and the other engaging in the military operations.

In time-honoured tradition, Pericles' death ushered in an era of competition, with rivals fighting to fill the space he left behind.

Pericles' successors did the exact opposite to him, and in other matters which apparently had no connection with the [Peloponnesian] war, private ambition and private profit led to policies which were bad for both the Athenians themselves and for their allies. Such policies, when successful, only brought credit and advantage to individuals, and when they failed, the whole potential of the state in the war was impaired.

What follows in Thucydides' account is similar to the argument that monarchists generally give, even today, in support of having a single leader who is born into power, and therefore not under any necessity to fight for it:

> The reason was that he [Pericles], influential by both his reputation and his judgement and known for being beyond corruptibility, held control of the masses independently. He led the masses rather than was led by them, and because he never had to flatter them in order to seek power by improper means, his prestige was such that he could anger them by contradicting them.[32]

Crowds are capricious, however – as we know, the Athenians punished Pericles for the power he held, before taking him back again, like the abused girlfriend in a never-ending relationship.

Foaming at the Mouth

Thucydides' description of the infighting among demagogues that followed Pericles' death has many modern incarnations – for example, the backstabbing fights for the Tory leadership in the wake of David Cameron's resignation in June 2016, or Theresa May's in May 2019. Almost any governing party in crisis, however, has experienced the same phenomenon, often in anticipation of the next window of demagogic opportunity. Political skulduggery is the whole premise of *House of*

Cards, a popular TV show that first aired in Britain in 1990, and returned with equal relevance as an American show in 2013. Even Cleisthenes, the founding father of democracy, in 508 BC became embroiled with other men fighting to secure influence in the power vacuum left by the tyrannicide of 510 BC. Herodotus tells us, 'these men with their factions fell to contending for power. Cleisthenes was getting the worst of it in this dispute, so he befriended the *demos*.'[33] The uncomfortable truth is that both demagoguery and good leadership require charm, the all-important ability to win over a crowd.

The public bear some responsibility for being manipulated by politicians who flatter them, and this is something the Athenians perhaps understood better than we do. The methods of Cleon, who rose to prominence in the 420s after Pericles' death in the plague, were ridiculed by his critics but remained successful in keeping the *demos* on side. First, he made a habit of expressing his hatred of the Athenian noble class, and made sure that any individuals who posed a potential threat to his influence became victims of the *sycophants*, who sent individuals to court on false charges (a specific type of political operator rather than the obsequious flatterer the term has come to mean today). Second, he was both an unrefined 'man of the people' and eloquent at the same time (President Erdoğan is an excellent comparison), and he used informers to keep himself in the know (modern methods of surveillance fulfil the same service). Third, he worked on the emotions of the Athenian populace whenever he spoke, and was repeatedly mocked for having a ridiculously bombastic style of oration, like President Erdoğan, who is often depicted on social media with a popular image of his furious red face, midway through a fiery speech. Last and most important, because money talks, he was responsible for increasing the pay for jury service by 50 per cent from two obols to three, solidifying his support amongst the poorer Athenian citizens.

Aristophanes is by far our most entertaining source on Cleon, and, more widely, insightful on the vanity of the *demos* and the ease with which it could be bought by any demagogue. Even if his plays were exaggerations of reality, they hit on some perennial truths. *The Knights* (performed in 424 BC) features rival demagogues who compete viciously and without shame in flattering the *demos* − literally a character called Demos − in order to defraud him. Demos has a slave who describes his master at the start of the play: 'We have a master, Demos, who lives on the Pnyx, boorish in temperament, a bean devourer quick to anger, an old sod who's impossible to please and going a bit deaf.'[34] (It is hard not to think of the image of Demos as an old man being crowned by the young woman Demokratia on the *stele* of 336 BC, almost a hundred years later, in a much more serious context.)

The slave also describes Demos's acquisition of a slave called Paphlagon (a caricature of the demagogue Cleon). 'This guy Paphlagon knows the old man's moods, he's a leather-seller, he kowtowed before his master, fawned, flattered, softened him up, and cheated him with little scraps of nothing.'[35] Paphlagon's name is a pun on *'paphlasdon'* – 'foaming at the mouth' – because Cleon was notoriously loud and spluttery. The only character worse than Paphlagon in *The Knights* is a rival caricature of a demagogue – a seller of guts and tripe, Agorakritos, literally 'Choice of the Marketplace'. In the end, Agorakritos usurps Paphlagon by being even more sycophantic to Demos.

PAPHLAGON: *O Demos, blow your nose, wipe it on my head.*
AGORAKRITOS: *No, on mine!*
PAPHLAGON: *No, on mine!*[36]

As a satirist, Aristophanes makes the audience as complicit as possible, both as participants in the action of the play and as citizens in the real world that is acknowledged beyond the stage. At one point in *The Knights*, the incumbent demagogue Paphlagon shouts to the audience: 'O venerable heliasts, fellow members of the brotherhood of the jurors' dole, whom I nourish by screeching about right and wrong – come to my rescue, I am being beaten up by conspirators!'[37]

Demagogues intimidate as much as they charm. Aristophanes gives us a hint of the fear that demagogues like Cleon wielded in Athenian society, even in the theatrical festivals: 'Don't worry: he is not represented in any portrait-mask, for out of fear of that man no one wanted to make his likeness. Doubtless he'll be recognized: the audience is clever.'[38] According to the much drier account of Thucydides, 'Cleon, son of Cleaenetus . . . was the most violent of the citizens and at that time by far the most persuasive to the people . . .'[39] It is still true today that violent and theatrical demagogues attract – rather than repel – crowds, because they subliminally convey a kind of macho strength to their audiences.

Erdoğan, Trump and Putin all display an excessively belligerent attitude towards critics both at home and abroad, but tend to get on well with each other – strong-birds of a feather. At a meeting between Trump and Modi at the White House in 2017, Modi declared: 'I am sure that convergence between my vision for "New India" and President Trump's vision to "Make America Great Again" will add new dimensions to our cooperation.'[40] Apart from any genuine feeling of kindred spirits, any calculating strongman who likes to break the rules understands that it is important to approve of the rule-breaking of others.

Make Athens Great Again

Some of our populists today are held back by checks and balances, like Trump; others less so, like Erdoğan. All claim to be democrats, but tend towards authoritarianism once in power, and what they have in common is the ability to command a mixture of fear and gratitude from their audiences. Sometimes it is not individuals who wield these emotions but more nebulous political movements, and there are populist parties which are more powerful than their individual leaders; in Italy, the Five Star Movement required merely an entertaining figurehead rather than a talented politician to tap into the conservative frustrations of a large swathe of the population. On the left, Podemos in Spain and Syriza in Greece profited from people's anger in the aftermath of the European debt crisis, promising to be different from the 'establishment' to win elections – this led to inevitable disappointment in both cases. But populist leaders and movements are not confined to left or right. President Macron of France came to power in 2017 as a centrist, promising to represent voters who felt squeezed out by the ever-polarizing parties of the left and right; within a couple of years, however, his nosediving popularity and particularly his out-of-touch response to the *gilets jaunes* (yellow vest protesters) of 2018 proved he was not quite the hero France thought he might be. The mystery of why centrist politicians are not more successful with modern electorates is perhaps based in the myth that most swing voters lie at the centre of the political spectrum; in fact, their views are likely to be much further to the left or right of the political representatives who are trying to court them, and this is what inspired the strategy of the Vote Leave campaign in Britain in 2016.

Stoking nostalgia for a superior, bygone era, while at the same time promising a bright new future, has always been a go-to tactic for conservative populists. In the fourth century BC, Demosthenes made a scathing attack on his audience at the Assembly as the forces of Macedon loomed, blaming them for being taken in by demagogues who had, in his view, dragged society down from its fifth-century heyday.

Why did everything go well then [in the fifth century] that now goes wrong? Because then the people, having the courage to act and to fight, controlled the politicians and were themselves the dispensers of all favours; the rest were well content to accept at the people's hand honour and authority and reward. Now, on the contrary, the politicians hold the purse-strings and manage everything, while you, the people, unnerved and stripped of wealth and of allies, have sunk to the level of lackeys and hangers-on, content if the politicians gratify you with a dole from the Theoric Fund or a procession at the Boëdromia, and your manliness reaches its climax when you add your thanks for what is your own. They have herded you up in the city and entice you with these baits, that they may keep you manageable and tamed.[41]

Demosthenes used a well-known strategy of idealizing the past, depicting the democracy of the fifth century as blessed by public speakers who were only interested in the common good, whereas in his time populism had taken over and had turned the people into idle subjects of these populists. Ironically, there was as much complaint in the fifth century BC as in Demosthenes' era in response to demagogues and the populist policies they advanced – as we saw, for example, in Aristophanes and his absurdist sketches of Paphlagon and Agorakritos abasing themselves before their master, Demos.

In fact, the Athenians were well aware that they could be carried away by demagogues who did not propose what was the most beneficial for the state; Demosthenes was not the first to point this out. In around 396 BC, the orator Lysias complained in a public court of law that 'what calls for the highest indignation is that the disposition of men in public life today is such that the orators do not propose what will be most beneficial to the city. You give your votes to proposals which bring profit to them.'[42] In ancient Athens, as now, a democracy must contend with the self-interest of people in power who have a more magnified voice than the multitude – this can manifest simply as proposing what will be popular to win votes (certain tax reductions, for example), but which will not necessarily 'be most beneficial to the city'. In more extreme cases, proposals or lobbying can be more directly self-serving – take, for example, the scramble among some Tories, previous Remainers, to back Brexit in 2016 as soon as it seemed the referendum might tip that way. Backing the right horse pays off.

Old Boys' Network

Given that there were no high positions of authority that commanded big salaries in ancient Athens, it is reasonable to question what exactly Lysias meant by 'profit'. Then, as now, holding political influence and generally being good at public speaking could be lucrative in various ways (receiving bribes for proposing a decree in the Assembly, for example, or getting paid to write speeches for wealthy defendants on trial), but aside from monetary gain, ambitious individuals could access wider-ranging influence and recognition just as they can today.

Mechanisms like the *kleroterion* ensured equal access to power on the most basic level, but Athenian citizens who were well educated and well connected would inevitably make more of such opportunities. Although anyone could stand on the speakers' platform at the Assembly and speak ('*ho boulomenos*'), there was a certain level of monopolization from an elite minority. The eloquence that was necessary to make an impact on a crowd of 6,000 people was based on formal training under sophists who were renowned for their rhetorical skills as well as their philosophical training – and the sophists cost money, as private schools do today. As the fifth century turned into the fourth, professionalism became more prominent in this sphere, as it did in most areas of public life, and being trained in oration would come in very handy either in speaking persuasively in the Assembly or on the Council of Five Hundred, influencing the deliberation which resulted in the preliminary decisions (*probouleumata*).

The most obvious modern parallel of an elite education leading to political success is in Britain. In the last three hundred years, forty out of fifty-four prime ministers have gone to Oxford or Cambridge University, and twenty have gone to Eton College – it is not merely the quality of the education of schools like Eton that sustain alumni in political life but the social networks they offer. In Athens, social cliques formed in the Agora, particularly in the major stoa (colonnade) hangouts, as well as at symposia (elite dinner parties), which also gave rise to rival philosophical and literary clubs. An important aspect of shaping the political identity of the Athenian youth would have been membership of associations or clubs, and demagogues were an unfortunate development of these, alongside Athens' broader culture of public speaking.

The general Alcibiades was a notorious member of one of the most elite clubs of fifth-century Athens; in Plato's famous work the *Symposium*, the philosopher records one of the parties attended by Alcibiades, Socrates, his hopeless admirer (and teacher), and the comic poet Aristophanes, at which they all discussed the origin of love. In 415 BC, Alcibiades, with supreme and unwarranted confidence, proposed to the Assembly the invasion of Sicily, which significantly turned the tide of a twenty-seven-year war that would eventually end in Spartan victory. One night as the expedition was being prepared in Athens, the city's *herms* (stone blocks which marked distances on roads, featuring the head of Hermes – the god of travel – and a phallus at the appropriate height), were found mysteriously mutilated – the phalluses had been chopped off, which many took as a bad omen that doomed the expedition to failure. Several people were accused, but the blame ultimately fell on Alcibiades who was notoriously prone to drunken rampages and had well-known oligarchic sympathies. He was recalled to Athens to stand trial as soon as he arrived in Sicily. Instead of returning, he defected to Sparta where he could finally enjoy living in a functioning oligarchy.

Alcibiades' profaning of the phallus and of religious rituals known as the Mysteries, cannot help but conjure up the antics of the Bullingdon Club of Oxford University, an elite social club whose wealthy young members have for centuries ritually vandalized other people's property in drunken, Bacchanalian stupors. Past members include former prime minister David Cameron, former chancellor of the exchequer George Osborne, and current prime minister Boris Johnson, who in 2013 admitted his membership of the club was a 'truly shameful vignette of almost superhuman undergraduate arrogance, toffishness and twittishness. But at the time you felt it was wonderful to be going round swanking it up.'[43]

Random acts of vandalism aside, however, Athens let their politicians get away with much less than we do today – the penalties not just for corruption but for bad policy-making were incredibly severe. Speakers in the Assembly were answerable for their speeches, especially when they put to vote motions which subsequently became decrees. It would have taken a great deal of gumption to propose either to the Council of Five Hundred or to the Assembly anything that was false, inaccurate or ill-motivated, or in any way 'not to the benefit of the people' (a crime that was regarded as treason), because the risk of being prosecuted was high. If you were convicted of misleading the people, at the very least your property would be confiscated, your citizenship could be revoked or you would be executed without further ado.

The problem of Athens' orators was an interesting paradox. On the one hand, democracy could not function without the fundamental role of public speakers, but on the other, there was constant suspicion among the electorate that public speakers might not be proposing what was best for the people; this meant that almost all prominent politicians in ancient Athens were ostracized or punished at some point.

Keeping the Score: One-Way Ticket

Our modern society is of course different from Athens; mainstream and social media hugely affect the democratic process, both informing and disinforming the people. But just as populists like Trump make the most of having a platform on Twitter, the demagogues of Athens exploited the Pnyx, which commanded a captive audience of voters almost every week of the year, and the ample opportunities to spread disinformation, cajole voters or intimidate critics in the Agora and, via informants, throughout the city state. The more significant difference between modern and ancient democratic society was actually the penalties put in place to deter and punish demagogues who did this – Trump's ancient Athenian alter ego would have been impeached several times over by now, or more likely deported or executed.

The path from demagogue to tyrant, even in the modern age, is a well-trodden one. The demagogue, having charmed his way into power, then becomes afraid of losing it, and uses increasingly desperate methods to suppress any opposition – just like Hippias becoming caught in a vicious cycle of cruelty and paranoia after the murder of his brother in 514 BC. The

Philippines, Venezuela, Russia, Turkey – the parallels are all too present today. The ancient Athenians were extremely conscious of the power of populists and their propensity towards tyranny, so they developed stringent methods to prevent that progression.

Imagine if we could vote to cast politicians we didn't like out of the country for ten years. Likely candidates in recent years include world leaders who have won elections but have also become increasingly unpopular and who could probably win the vote for the most hated or feared politician in their respective countries (provided the vote was secret). We know that in the fifth century BC, politicians who won the 'most unwanted' vote – a little like a Razzie Award for Worst Actor – were cast out of Athens for ten years thanks to a practice called ostracism. Counter-intuitively, it was not always the most unpopular or most hated public figure that got exiled – often the fear was that an individual was becoming too popular and thus becoming too powerful for democracy to contain. We know exactly who the main contenders for this dubious honour were because thousands of the ballots bearing the names of nominees and winners have survived.

The ancient equivalent of scrap paper was sherds (fragments of old pots); citizens wrote the name of the public figure they wanted exiled onto a sherd, which then known as an ostrakon, and submitted it, with the writing facing downwards, to be counted. After all the ostraka were counted and the "winner" announced, the sherds would be shovelled up and used to fill in potholes in the roads near the Agora. Luckily, these deposits were well preserved and have been dug up by archaeologists during excavations. The names on some of them match the people we know were ostracized from literary sources – Aristeides 'The Just', Themistocles the hero of Salamis, creator of the Athenian navy and builder of the city's protective walls, Kimon the son of Miltiades, hero of Marathon. Even Pericles himself was a candidate for ostracism but did not 'win' (he probably would have done if he had not died prematurely in the plague in 429 BC). It would not be an exaggeration to say that almost every popular politician mentioned in ancient sources was at some point ostracized – surprisingly, this did not seem to deter ambitious would-be leaders of the fifth century BC.

Even by Athenian standards, ostracism seems a needlessly harsh check on power; Cleisthenes introduced the practice in 508/7 BC, just after the fall of tyranny (although it was not implemented until after the Persian Wars) as a measure designed to pre-emptively protect democracy by preventing the rise of potential tyrants. The problem was that ostracism, unlike the classic form of Athenian voting (show of hands), or the *kleroterion*, was open to fraud. Many of the names scratched into the ostraka that survive today are written in similar handwriting (including a huge number with Themistocles' name on them), which suggests they were prepared in advance. This could perhaps have been legal; many Athenians may have been illiterate, and would have needed someone else to write for them (some of the sherds that have survived carry misspelled names). However, such a large number of pre-inscribed ballots bearing Themistocles' name in almost identical handwriting suggests a political opponent at work.

The practice of preparing and entering ostraka for a particular candidate would have been similar to the tactics used by rival political parties ahead of national elections in large and polarized democracies like Turkey, which insist on referring to themselves as democracies despite evidence (bins full of pre-stamped ballots) to the contrary. Nigeria's attempted solution to voter impersonation and multiple votes being cast by the same person has been a new electronic system. It works by giving election officials a handheld device which verifies a voter's identity card in a two-step authentication process, in a way that is becoming common with digital banking. Even more impressively, the handheld devices can be programmed to work only at certain times and locations, and to transmit but not receive data, to reduce the possibility of a hack.

But as is often the case, there are other factors at play when elections are hotly contested, and the elections in February 2019 were subject to the same claims of electoral fraud as usual: ballots can still be stolen or substituted after being cast, and people can still be bribed or intimidated – either into not using the electronic verification system, in the case of the election officials, or into voting a certain way, in the case of the voters themselves. There is only so much scope for outwitting or outspending human interference with digital devices. The only thing that can counter undemocratic tendencies is the opposite: the democratic spirit of people determinedly sleeping with their arms around ballot boxes to physically prevent them from being stolen (as happened in Turkey in 2014 and 2019), the spirit of opposition candidates brave enough to stand against entrenched authoritarian leaders, and those voters brave enough to vote for them despite intimidation. In the end, only courage works – and even then, it is often not enough.

By the end of the fifth century BC, ostracism had been abandoned; ironically, a system designed to rid democracy of unfair influence itself became an instrument of just that. And yet, arguably, desperate times call for desperate measures. Just in case anyone might wish to reintroduce ostracism today, the process has been conveniently described for us by Philochorus, a Greek historian of the third century BC – he tells us it happened every year if needed, mentions a quorum of 6,000 votes to condemn any candidate to exile (the same as for a public vote), and describes the terms of the exile itself. There is no mention of precautions to check the ostracized man did not return before his ten years were up; he would have been so well known that his face would be instantly recognizable before he got into town, much like the faces of politicians that are far too familiar to us from the front pages of tabloid newspapers and Twitter screens.

Ostracism takes place as follows. The people vote on whether it is necessary to hold an ostracism, before the eighth prytany [five-week term of governance, ten per year]. If it is necessary, the agora is fenced in with boards, leaving ten entrances, through which the people enter in their tribes, and deposit their sherds with the writing facing downwards. The nine archons and the council of five hundred oversee the process. When the sherds have been counted to determine who has the most votes (which must be not less than 6,000), then this person must, after settling his personal commitments, leave the city within ten days, for a period of ten years [this was later reduced to five years]. He is allowed to receive income from his possessions, but he must not come nearer [to Athens] than Geraestum, the headland on Euboea [an island off Attica].[44]

It is remarkable how finely balanced major national elections and referendums have been in the past few years: the Leave camp won the Brexit referendum by a margin of less than 2 per cent in June 2016; Donald Trump received 2.1 million fewer votes than Hillary Clinton but won a majority of electoral votes in November 2016; and in April 2019, Ekrem Imamoğlu, an opponent of President Erdoğan's ruling party, was elected mayor of Istanbul by fewer than 14,000 votes (he later won again in the June re-run by a much bigger margin). This is partly due to the deeply divisive nature of the politicians themselves, certainly in the case of figures like Trump. Today, ostracism really would shake things up. On purely numerical grounds, more people despise than love Trump, for example, as suggested by the popular vote and subsequent approval ratings, so his exile – perhaps to Mexico – would be almost guaranteed.

Neck on the Line

It is always a challenge to keep politicians accountable, especially now that ostracism is no longer in vogue. Roman engineers were said to stand underneath the bridges they had constructed so that when the supports were removed, they would have been crushed immediately if the structure collapsed. This may be an urban legend but there is a more feasible model to emulate in the example of the architects of Ephesus, as described by the Roman architect and engineer Vitruvius, who wrote a treatise on architecture dedicated to the Emperor Augustus in the 20s BC. In this he writes of his admiration for the law of Ephesus, which dictates that when an architect accepts a commission he estimates the cost, and his own property is pledged as security until completion of the project. If the finished cost aligns with his estimate, he is rewarded and honoured – if more than an additional 25 per cent has been spent, the money is taken from the architect's property. 'Would to God that this were also a law of the Roman people!' says Vitruvius, admiringly.

The ancient Athenians were excessively disciplinarian in their approach to powerful individuals who stepped out of line. Telling lies or making false promises in the Assembly was 'misleading the people', and could lead to *eisangelia* (impeachment). Specified in the law relating to impeachment is the offence of 'being a rhetor and not speaking what is best for the Athenian *demos*'. There are plenty of politicians in democracies all over the world who could well be accused of 'not speaking what is best for the *demos*' – especially those involved in the Brexit debate. However, in Britain at least, there has not been a single prosecution to date over a politician lying about a matter of public policy in an election campaign.

And yet, such is the fury to which ordinary British citizens have been driven by Brexit, a private *eisangelia* was launched in 2016 against Boris Johnson, who stoked outlandish fears that Turkey would soon be joining the EU and would flood the UK with migrants, and promoted the infamous claim that £350 million could be saved from weekly payments to the EU and diverted to the National Health Service.

Marcus Ball is a private citizen who has been on a mission to prosecute Johnson for the alleged offence of misconduct in office. 'If we could win a prosecution against such immoral and untrustworthy actions [as Johnson's promotion of the NHS claims] the precedent could make it illegal for them to occur in future,' Ball explained.[45] On 29 May 2019, Johnson was ordered to appear in Westminster magistrates court, but the High Court threw the case out shortly afterwards. Ball's prosecution was highly unusual; British office holders prosecuted for misconduct generally behave badly in secret – the 2018 investigation into bullying and sexual harassment in Westminster in the wake of the *#MeToo* movement being a case in point (the names of the MPs under investigation were also kept secret, which the Athenians would never have allowed). Debating policy, even if it is ill-intentioned or dishonest policy, is something done openly, with plenty of witnesses. If politicians became afraid to debate policy because they might be accused of 'not speaking what is best for the *demos*', it might stifle political debate completely – though it certainly did not seem to in Athens.

Statistically speaking, the number of statesmen, generals and politicians who were charged for offences and fined, disenfranchised, ostracized or executed in ancient Athens is daunting – in fact the majority of them had to suffer one of those penalties at some point in their life. Unlike other forms of governments in antiquity, Athenian democracy was characterized by both the frequency of political prosecutions and the litigiousness of the people.

Times have changed, however. We still have self-interested, deceitful politicians, but not nearly such a strong culture of punishment, which is both good and bad. A system of deterrence more in keeping with the modern age might be to introduce something like the Advertising Standards Authority (ASA) to political campaigning. The ASA is a self-regulating body to which almost all companies that advertise in the UK voluntarily sign up. It defines its own operations as follows:

We respond to concerns and complaints from consumers and businesses and take action to ban ads which are misleading, harmful, offensive or irresponsible. As well as responding to complaints we monitor ads to check they're following the rules. We also conduct research to test public opinion and identify where we need to take action to protect consumers.[46]

Among the rules on misleading ads set out on the ASA's website, the following apply most pertinently to the Vote Leave campaign claims: 'Rule 3.3: Marketing communications must not mislead the consumer by omitting material information. They must not mislead by hiding material information or presenting it in an unclear, unintelligible, ambiguous or untimely manner.'[47] Likewise: 'Rule 3.17: Price statements must not mislead by omission, undue emphasis or distortion. They must relate to the product featured in the marketing communication.'

The £350 million NHS bus is unlikely to have passed those tests, so that people like Marcus Ball would not have to go to the trouble of bringing unsuccessful *eisangeliai* against people like Boris Johnson, who seems to be a magnet for legal threats. The barrister Jo Maugham QC, well known for having brought legal challenges against the Brexit process, also launched a scathing attack on Johnson on Twitter just four days before Britain's intended date for departing the EU on 29 March 2019: 'It is time the tax-dodging wealthy foreign newspaper proprietors [including presumably the Barclay brothers, owners of the *Daily Telegraph*, for which Johnson writes regularly] stopped printing their lies. It is time the BBC stopped broadcasting their lies. It is time you and I started calling out their lies. @*BorisJohnson* you are a liar. Now sue me, I dare you.'[48]

Brexit brings out the ancient Athenian spirit in us all.

Day of Reckoning

As far as we know, there were no organized protest movements in Athens as there are today, although there were moments of mass hysteria and outrage, like the public's reaction to the generals' conduct at Arginusae. The ways in which we attempt to punish our politicians – either by organizing protests, or by not voting for them in an election – would have seemed laughably inadequate to the Athenian *demos*. Instead, their statesmen and magistrates were subjected to a sophisticated and targeted matrix of laws dedicated to punishing those who abused power. There were even rules in place to check on those in office (including all members of the Council of Five Hundred) before and after their term in office – the *dokimasia* (pre-check) and the *euthyna* (post-check), which is still the modern Greek word for 'responsibility'. Ancient public officials were effectively frisked by the overzealous security guards of the legal system and the tiniest bleep would condemn them to trial.

Modern scandals involving misconduct in office, like the scandal which followed the *Daily Telegraph*'s publication in 2009 of British MPs' abuse of expenses, leading to resignations, repayments, sackings and in some cases jail terms for members of the House of Commons and House of Lords, pale in comparison to the rigours the Athenian *demos* applied to their public officials. In fact, that particular scandal would never have happened, because expenses would never have been privately recorded anyway (it was a 2008 Freedom of Information Request that started the chain of events that led to their publication) and the MPs in question would not have gone undetected for years; more sobering yet, if it had happened, even the more minor offenders would have been executed.

While ostracism was a proactive measure to prevent public figures becoming too powerful, most measures against misconduct in public office in Athens were reactive and incredibly draconian, certainly not to be emulated in our times. The two best known were the law of the *graphe paranomon*, which was prosecution for introducing an illegal proposal to the people, and the law of *eisangelia*, i.e. impeachment, when there was a serious charge such as treason or corruption. The accuser, who could be any citizen (like Marcus Ball), could denounce someone in the Assembly or the Council of Five Hundred for having committed offences such as 'subverting democracy', serious offences in the military sphere, or deception of the people by an orator. Demosthenes conjures up the outrage of the crowd responding to a lying politician, and the reluctance to give him a second chance:

> *When a man, then, felt no shame in deceiving you to whom he had pledged his word, though there are laws which declare that, if a man deceives the people by a promise, he shall be liable to impeachment — when, after swearing and imprecating destruction upon himself, he had no fear of the gods in whose name he had perjured himself — was it strange that I was unwilling to allow him to take an oath?* [49]

Every year, the principal Assembly in the sixth *prytany* (i.e. the sixth out of the ten political terms in the year), would be designated to hold votes on all the cases connected to disruptive or dangerous behaviour of citizens and politicians. This day of reckoning would deal with the following: (1) a decision had to be taken on whether to hold an ostracism or not; (2) the public prosecutions against sycophants would receive preliminary decisions; (3) decisions would be taken on whether any politician had made a promise to the people and not fulfilled it.

It is impressive – if a little terrifying – to see how obsessed the Athenians were with protecting their own democratic system from systemic threats, like a human organism in the grip of an autoimmune attack. But if they were overzealous in tackling perceived threats, we are not zealous enough. Expenses scandals are one thing, and election promises are broken all the time – it would be impossible and indeed dangerous to police the latter. But there have been some major cases of misconduct in office happening in plain sight in recent decades, like George Bush and Tony Blair's reckless decision (some say even criminally so) to invade Iraq in 2003. (After instigating Britain's role in this invasion, Blair worked as the UN's special Middle East peace envoy for eight years, during which time he achieved nothing of note.) When world leaders make appallingly far-reaching mistakes, and are not only forgiven but lauded and given further positions of power, we should realize we have a serious problem with holding our politicians to account.

Lesson Three:
Think Again

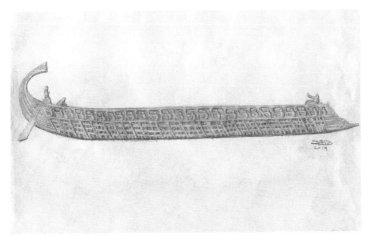

An Athenian trireme, or warship, icon of Athenian overseas power.
(Acropolis Museum, Athens)

Democracy always has a major advantage over non-democratic society. It has the capacity for self-correction. And in my view, the major crisis of democracy is when it starts to lose the capacity for self-correction.

IVAN KRASTEV[50]

135

In 428 BC, the Mytilenians of Lesbos wanted to relinquish their membership of the Delian League, an alliance of city states which paid Athens taxes and provided warships in return for protection against Persia. The Mytilenians resented these obligations, so they staged a revolt. It was crushed, and the furious Athenians held a vote on whether to exterminate the entire male population of the island and enslave the women and children in revenge. The vote carried, and a trireme was immediately dispatched to Mytilene, the main port of Lesbos, to carry out the deed.

But the next day, as Thucydides records:

> . . . they felt immediate remorse and reflection at their cruel and savage decree to condemn the entire city rather than just those that merited it. When the Mytilenian envoys and their Athenian sympathizers saw this, they asked the authorities to reopen the issue to a vote; they were easily persuaded, because the authorities themselves saw that clearly the majority of citizens wanted someone to allow them to reconsider the issue. There was an assembly called immediately.[51]

Diodotus, the leading proposer of a second vote, argued his case to overturn the original decision not on the grounds of clemency, but of rationale. It was not in Athens' best interests to kill all the Mytilenians, he said; a softer option would be more beneficial for both sides.

At the end of a day of vigorous debate, it was agreed that

ballots should be cast a second time. The counting of hands was a nerve-wracking moment: 'The two opinions were most evenly matched, and the Athenians, notwithstanding their change in feeling, went straight to voting and the final show of hands was nearly evenly matched, but Diodotus' motion prevailed.' However, time had passed and there was no way of knowing whether the original trireme had already reached Lesbos – suddenly, everyone was gripped by the horrific realization that perhaps the second vote had come too late to save the Mytilenians.

At once they sent out another trireme in great haste, lest they find the city destroyed because the first ship had already arrived, it having already a day and a night's head start. Wine and barley were provided for the ship by the Mytilenian envoys, who also promised great rewards if they made it in time. The zeal was so high during the voyage that they ate barley kneaded with wine and oil while they rowed, and took turns sleeping while others rowed . . .

Thucydides tells us that the ship arrived just after the first decree had been read out to the assembled Mytilenians. The crowd would have just had time to digest the chilling news before the second ship pulled into port, urgent shouts coming from the men on board to stop the impending massacre. 'This was how close the Mytilenians came to destruction.'

The Mytilenian Debate shows us that it is not the first time that an initial decision has come to seem hasty, or regrettable. After June 2016, many in Britain wished for the equivalent of a faster trireme to save the day as the Article 50 time bomb ticked away. The arguments that gripped Britain about whether a second referendum would be the right course of action have all been had before; in fact, it is possible to reproduce the debate verbatim from Thucydides and substitute modern terms to see just how uncannily history repeats itself.

Here is the most relevant text: part of the speech made by Diodotus, in which 'Brexit' has been substituted for variations on 'executing the Mytilenians'. Diodotus, who opposed the first decision to execute the Mytilenians and wanted another vote, is the equivalent of a Remainer, arguing for a second referendum on Brexit; his opponent, Cleon, is a Brexiteer, adamantly opposed to a second referendum. Athens is Britain, and Mytilene is the EU (the original story of course was the other way round, with Mytilene wanting to leave the Delian League – one of the occupational hazards of historical parallels). Imagine the speech taking place in front of the entire electorate – perhaps an address to camera.

'I do not blame those who have proposed to bring up again the decision about [Brexit], nor do I commend those who say it is a bad thing to frequently deliberate on matters of importance. I consider the greatest obstacles to wise counsel to be haste and anger: haste usually involves folly; anger usually involves ignorance and shallow reasoning . . .

'But it is right to expect we who discuss matters of the greatest importance ought to take a longer view than you who just look at

the issues briefly, especially since we are held accountable for giving our advice, but you are not held accountable for listening to it. For if the man who gave advice and the man who took it suffered equally, you would consider things more moderately. But as it is, whenever some passion leads you to disaster, you only punish the judgement of your adviser and not your own judgement, even if many share responsibility for the error.

'I consider our deliberations to be more about the future than the present . . .

'I ask you not to reject what is useful in my proposal just because of what is attractive in his. His proposal may seem more just to you in your present anger against the [EU]. But we are not sitting as jurors in a court of justice, but considering in an assembly how the [European Union] might be of use to [Britain].

'Hope and desire — the one leading, the other following; the one thinking up the scheme, the other suggesting how to accomplish it — wreak the greatest damage, and though invisible have more power than perils that can be seen. Fortune, too, adds to the incitement, and by the unexpected aid that she sometimes lends Fortune tempts men to run risks even when they are in inferior positions—men, and states. Because it is with states that the stakes are the highest: freedom, or the power to control others. And when acting together each individual irrationally thinks himself greater. In short, it is impossible to prevent (and foolish to believe differently) human nature from doing what it has eagerly set its mind upon, by force of law or by any other means of deterrence.

'Therefore, we must not choose inferior policies by trusting in [Brexit] as a safeguard . . .

'And here too, consider how misguided you would be by following Cleon's counsel . . .

Such was Diodotus' speech. The two opinions were most evenly matched, and [the British electorate], notwithstanding their change in feeling, went straight to voting and the final show of hands was nearly evenly matched, but Diodotus' motion prevailed.

Debates raged in Britain in private households, in the media and in Parliament over whether or not to call a second referendum on Brexit, intensifying in the months leading up to the original date fixed for departure (29 March 2019). The arguments against it ranged from matters of practicality (there would be no time to prepare, hold and act on a referendum before that date), to constitutional worries about voting twice on the same issue, and confusion over what the wording of the referendum question would be: Leave vs. Remain, like the first time? Leave vs. Theresa May's Deal? Or, most controversial of all, a three-option referendum: Remain vs. Theresa May's Deal vs. No Deal? The lack of an obvious answer seemed daunting, and even some Remainers argued that a second referendum would be wrong in principle, setting a dangerous precedent – why would anyone bother to vote or expect their vote to be respected in future if referendums could just be repeated?

Yet individual cases can be compelling. Switzerland made history in 2019 by annulling the result of a referendum for the first time since it introduced the practice in 1848: the Supreme Court decided that a 2016 vote on amending tax laws to avoid penalizing married couples was not legitimate because voters had been misinformed by the official information given out (the number of married couples adversely affected by the existing tax law was given as 80,000, but the real figure was 454,000). The Christian Democrat party, which had proposed the change in policy that was put to the public, lodged an appeal against the result (which was an extremely narrow defeat – 49.2 to 50.8 per cent) and won. In the case of the Brexit referendum, no party has lodged an official appeal to annul the result, despite Vote Leave being found guilty of breaking electoral law (not for lying, but for overspending on its campaign), and the pressure to repeat the vote has come more from the public than from political representatives – there has been no figure quite as compelling as Diodotus speaking from the podium.

From Thucydides' retelling, it is easy to see why Diodotus succeeded in convincing the Athenian public that a second vote on Mytilene would be a good idea – particularly as most of them already supported the idea. He pointed out that the original decision was motivated primarily by emotion, which is also true of Brexit. The Vote Leave campaign appealed to generic feelings of nostalgia for a bygone era of perceived sovereignty – 'take back control' – and a mistrust of foreigners (tens of millions of Turks poised to flood the UK), while the Remain campaign put its trust in facts and figures, and a drier appeal to the status quo. But feelings, as Diodotus points out, generally win over reason, particularly when a debate becomes polarized. Indeed, as the referendum drew closer, the Remain camp became guilty of playing the Vote Leave camp at its own game by stoking emotions; the projections of economic doom that came to be known as 'Project Fear', while much more realistic than the disingenuous predictions of Turkey's entry to the EU employed by Vote Leave, also attempted to leverage public anxiety about the prospect of leaving – with less success, of course.

Dominic Cummings, who ran the Vote Leave campaign, was immediatly appointed senior advisor to Boris Johnson when he became Prime Minister in July 2019. When we interviewed him for his book in March of the same year, he was unapologetic about his running of the campaign, arguing that he was merely tapping into what the British public wanted. He was also scathing about the attempts of Tory politicians to negotiate a Brexit deal in the post-2016 period.

'If you'd taken twenty-five random people three years ago, after the referendum result, and put them in charge of Brexit, they would have done a much better job than these clowns,' he told us – a resounding endorsement of sortition. A keen student of ancient history, and in particular of Thucydides, Cummings is also a fan not only of sortition but of Athenian legislature: "[There was a] virtue in the ancient Athenians having relatively simple laws – I think a great constitutional change would be for laws to be read out a in Parliament so that everyone knew what they were voting on. He agrees with the concept of reconsidering an initial referendum result – 'the voting public can and should change their mind' – but points out that a second Brexit referendum was explicitly ruled out before June 2016. Any attempts to wrangle a second referendum after that, he says, would have been cheating.

I wrote in 2015 about how a process for two referendums would be more rational than the entire foolish approach of [David] Cameron. All the top Remainers – Cameron, Osborne, Clegg, the official Remain campaign and so on – said, 'No way, Cummings, no tricks, just one vote; it's for a generation, we all promise to implement the result, and Leave means out of the Single Market and Customs Union.' They said this because they were sure they would win and they wanted to crush the enemy. But having promised 'just one vote and we'll respect the result', they now say they want a rematch. But they either do not understand how badly this damages trust in democracy – much more than half the country think the MPs [would be] just cancelling a vote they don't like – or else they know but don't care. The best argument for a second referendum is that it would destroy all the existing parties, and I guarantee you that if it happens the People's Vote gang [a contingent of those in favour of a second Brexit referendum] will get a dreadful shock.

The Mytilenian Debate remains illuminating in its parallels to the original Brexit referendum. Diodotus' points about hope, greediness and haste are painfully relevant to the motivations of

Leave voters: the hope that the UK would be better off outside the EU, the willingness to believe in the fictional rebate of £350 million per week back into the UK's coffers, the haste which meant that Article 50 was triggered before it needed to be, setting the UK on a course to exit the EU too soon. Most importantly, we can recognize his appeal to acknowledge the 'false belief' that can lead to a terrible decision, and the importance of changing course accordingly. His speech is a wordy way of saying, 'This is a moment for self-correction,' the greatest virtue of democracy as encapsulated by the political scientist Ivan Krastev.

Family Therapy

The ability to self-reflect and self-correct is usually applied to individuals, not society. It is often difficult enough to acknowledge one's own mistakes, let alone a collective mistake – it brings blame and embarrassment, especially in a group scenario when there are always others to blame, and pride to protect. Denial sets in, and becomes entrenched. Collective self-correction, in fact, sounds uncomfortably like family therapy when considered in these terms, an awkward process that most people understandably avoid. It is easier to open up the capacity for changing course if it becomes standard practice to test initial decisions, though that is of course a slippery slope. There are some inspiring ancient precedents, however – Herodotus tells us that voting twice was common practice in fifth-century Persian society, employing the ageless principle of *in vino veritas*. The practice would probably only be popular today in the wine-loving inner circles of Brussels, but does give pause for thought.

> *Moreover, it is their custom to deliberate about the gravest matters when they are drunk; and what they approve in their deliberations is proposed to them the next day, when they are sober, by the master of the house where they deliberate; and if, being sober, they still approve it, they act on it, but if not, they drop it. And if they have deliberated about a matter when sober, they decide upon it when they are drunk.*[52]

The Athenians did not generally waste time agonizing over past decisions, and certainly did not make a practice of voting twice on the same issue. Then, as now, overturning a law or a decree risked undermining the *raison d'être* of laws, which is to remain unchanged and guarantee order and civility. Important decisions were often given special legal protection to prevent them from being changed, known as entrenchment clauses, which in fact shows it was not illegal to put to a second vote something which had already been decided – but it did have to follow a certain procedure. In the case of the Mytilenian Debate, the situation was acknowledged to be an emergency, and there was enough popular support for a second vote to make it possible for the *prytaneis* (presiding committee of the Council) to speed up the usual cumbersome legal steps to allow this to happen ('the authorities themselves saw clearly that most of the citizens wanted someone to give them a chance to reconsider the matter. So an Assembly was called at once').

Sometimes an emergency can lead to panicked bending of the rules. In the House of Commons, a mere ten days before Britain was due to exit the EU on 29 March 2019, the deal negotiated by Theresa May had already been put to MPs twice, and they had twice voted it down – yet it was due to be voted on a third time, an ironic development given May's own insistence that a second referendum on Brexit would be undemocratic. The House of Commons Speaker, John Bercow, caused great controversy by attempting to block the possibility of a third vote, saying that the question 'may not be brought forward again during the same session', and adding that this was a 'strong and long-standing convention' dating back to 1604. Bercow noted that the convention (which he called a 'rule') had been confirmed repeatedly throughout British political history: in 1864, 1870, 1882, 1891 and 1912. Yet Bercow has, at other times, been less keen on observing convention. In January 2019, he supported Remain MPs in their bid to force May to present a different Brexit plan shortly after she lost her first vote. 'If we always went by precedent, manifestly nothing in our procedures would ever change,' he said on that occasion.

'Self-correction' comes in many forms – flouting precedent or indeed rewriting the rule book – but the tendency of a democracy is to repeat the same old mistakes. In the end, the success of democracy comes down to the ability between opponents to compromise, and to avoid stalemate and rancour.

The spectacular failure of both the Conservative and Labour Parties to achieve any coherent policy regarding Brexit from 2016 onwards was the family fall-out that no amount of hypothetical therapy could fix.

The Sicilian Expedition

The initial vote of the Mytilenian Debate was not the only terrible decision questioned in fifth-century Athens. In 415 BC, the mood of the public concerning the ongoing Peloponnesian War was bullish, despite the peace treaty technically in place – the year before, Athenian forces had razed one of Sparta's allies, the island of Melos, to the ground. The time was ripe for generals to push in favour of a major military expedition to Sicily, which was in the grip of civil war. Envoys from one of the Sicilian factions had come to Athens asking for help, painting a picture of easy victory. In fact, the expedition was colossally ambitious with a very high chance of failure, as acknowledged by Athens' more cautious and experienced generals.

Alcibiades, the über-confident, good-looking pupil of Socrates and self-styled star of the military and of aristocratic society, proposed to lead the expedition, for reasons that were mainly personal, as Thucydides tells us:

The most passionate advocate of the expedition was Alcibiades, son of Cleinias, who desired to oppose Nicias [an older and more experienced general], as he was both at odds with Nicias politically in other matters and had previously been slandered by him; he [Alcibiades] was most especially eager to take command, and he hoped that through his efforts he could conquer Sicily and Carthage, and at the same time add to his own personal wealth and reputation.[53]

The Athenian people were sold on Alcibiades' proposal, and voted to allow the expedition, so a decree was immediately issued to send sixty ships under the command of three generals: Nicias (who, ironically, was against the expedition and had not wanted to be chosen), Alcibiades himself, and Lamachus. A second meeting of the Assembly was held five days later, which was meant to discuss the preparations for the expedition, but Nicias hijacked it by giving a speech in which he attempted to persuade the Athenians not to undertake the expedition at all: 'This assembly was convened to consider the preparations to be made for sailing to Sicily. But I think we still ought to further consider the decision itself, whether it's a good idea to send out ships at all . . .'[54]

During the months of negotiations on the terms of Britain's exit from the EU, despite the usual taboo on questioning the 2016 referendum's decision, many members of the public (although relatively few MPs) suggested that perhaps a rethink would be sensible, as the problems of exiting the EU became clearer than they had been at the time of the vote. Arguably, both the decision to go ahead with the Sicilian Expedition and the decision to go ahead with Brexit were taken on the basis of disinformation peddled by those who were pushing for the 'Invade/Leave' option. Given that Theresa May originally campaigned for Remain in 2016, before becoming prime minister after David Cameron's resignation, it would be logical to assume that, deep down, she opposed Brexit, just as Nicias opposed the Sicilian Expedition, though his job was to lead it. The parallel ends there, however; May sought the leadership of the Conservative Party, and with it the responsibility for dealing with Brexit – Nicias did not seek the leadership of the Sicilian Expedition. Moreover, May was always determined to deliver Brexit, and was emphatically against a second referendum, while Nicias asked the *prytanis*, the official who was presiding at the meeting, to allow discussion in the Assembly on whether they should go ahead with the expedition at all, while showing full awareness that this was a controversial request.

And you, president of the assembly, if you think it your duty to take care for the city's interests and to be a good citizen, call another vote, put the question again to the Athenians, and if you are afraid to call for a re-vote, remember that you cannot be charged with a violation of the law when there are so many witnesses on your side, and consider that you will become the healer of the city's counsels, that this will be considered good governance: a man who serves his country as he best can, and does it no harm intentionally.

It is significant that Nicias appealed to a duty of care on the part of those in charge. If the *prytanis* was worried about 'overturning' the decree passed at the previous meeting of the Assembly, Nicias assured him that he would not be charged with violating the laws because there were so many witnesses, implying that the number of people present in the Assembly was enough of a legitimization for this course of action. This has been an argument more or less made throughout Brexit also – that the sheer number of people arguing for a rethink on the decision to leave the EU (and indeed the close result – 52/48 per cent – of the referendum) legitimized a 'people's vote', despite the fact that there was no necessity for this under the law.

Nevertheless, Nicias' speech shows us he was aware that it was borderline illegal – or certainly frowned upon – to vote on something already decided (an action summed up by the single word *anapsephizein* in ancient Greek). In the case of the Mytilenian Debate, the public support for a second vote must have been obvious to the *prytaneis* (presiding council) – the Athenian people as a mass were feeling guilt-ridden over their decision to massacre the Mytilenians. In the case of the Sicilian Expedition, however, the popular sentiment was not there to support Nicias' opinion and give the necessary legitimization to the *prytaneis* to put the matter to the vote again. Comparing the two cases, it would seem that the emotional state of the majority of the electorate must have made a huge difference in such cases, something that is less easy to discern today with enormous population sizes and the fact that the electorate is not physically present within the halls of power.

Only the One Country

In 416 BC, just a year before they voted for the Sicilian Expedition, the Athenians voted to kill all the men on the island of Melos (a former colony of Sparta), and sell all the women and children into slavery, just as they had initially voted to do to the Mytilenians in 427 BC. This time, however, there was no collective regret and no one suggested a second vote. The war had been going on for fifteen years by the time Melos came on the agenda, and the Athenians were desensitized to cruelty and corrupted by their desire for victory at whatever cost (see Lesson Five).

The Melian Dialogue is Thucydides' account of the failed negotiations between Melian and Athenian representatives after the Athenians had been harassing the Melians for some time, exacting tribute despite the fact that the Melians were not one of their allies. It has long been famous as an exercise in realpolitik, and for the Athenians' expression of the fact that they could do what they wanted because they were the more powerful party – 'The strong do what they can and the weak suffer what they must' (commonly but inaccurately characterized as the principle of 'might is right'). This came to have particular relevance in 2015 for modern Greeks during the bailout negotiations with the European Commission; an Athenian we interviewed reread the Melian Dialogue in 2018 and was startled by the similarities:

I was reminded of my emotions sitting in front of the TV in 2015, waiting to see the results of the bailout discussions [Germany refused to soften Greece's conditions]. I felt exactly the same emotions. Thucydides shows us how people think, what people do for money, for power, and how strong people always want to be stronger. It's a story that goes on and on – we can also see it in Europe and America today.

Greece's ex-finance minister Yanis Varoufakis clearly agreed; the title of his 2016 book decrying Germany's austerity measures contains a choice Thucydidean quotation: *And the Weak Suffer What They Must? Europe, Austerity and the Threat to Global Stability.*[55]

The Melian Dialogue of 416 BC is also one of the most striking of ancient Brexit comparisons, because it puts Britain into a decidedly unexpected victim role: that of Melos, a tiny but incredibly self-confident island that attempted to negotiate a good deal for itself instead of utter ruination against a much greater power (Athens/the EU). The Athenians repeatedly demanded that Melos surrender and agree to join the Delian League over the course of ten years, but the Melians steadfastly refused, claiming that they would never give up their sovereignty, and predicting that they would be rescued by Sparta in the nick of time anyway. At the same time, they demanded that the Athenians let them remain neutral (i.e. not officially allied to Sparta), leave them alone, and furthermore sign a treaty that would be more beneficial to the Melians. The Athenians explained to them that they had no negotiating position at all, and urged them to reconsider, but the Melians refused – so they were slaughtered.

As with the Mytilenian Debate, it is irresistibly easy to reproduce the Melian Dialogue as a summary of the negotiations between the British government and the EU in the lead-up to Britain's proposed exit from the EU in 2019, in particular the last exchange between the Athenians [the EU] and the astonishingly brazen Melians [the British]. The Athenians are amazed by the Melians' suicidal refusal to admit reality, and their faith in foreign allies coming to the rescue (similar to Britain's adamant belief that foreign treaties would make up for being kicked out of the Common Market).

'We are shocked that while you said that you would take counsel concerning your survival, you have said not one thing that gives men confidence to think that they will be saved. Rather your strongest arguments are what you hope lies in the future, whereas your actual resources are too insignificant to confront those resources arrayed against you. You will show a great lack of common sense unless, after we retire, you decide something more sensible than all of this. Surely you will not fall into that sense of disgrace that is most destructive for men facing shameful and manifest dangers. For in many cases, men have their eyes open to the dangers ahead of them, but this thing called disgrace, by the power of a seductive name, has drawn these men into a state where they have surrendered to the phrase, while in fact they fall willingly into hopeless

disaster, and earn for themselves a disgrace more shameful in folly than in misfortune.

'This, if you consider properly, you will guard against, and you will suppose that it is not unseemly to submit when the greatest city offers you reasonable terms, keeping your own territory as tributary allies, and not, when you are given the choice between war or security, favouring the worse option: as those who do not yield to their equals, who comport themselves well towards their superiors, and act moderately towards their inferiors, are most successful. Think it over, then, even after we've withdrawn, and keep this constantly in your mind, that you are deliberating about your country, concerning which a single country will depend on a single decision for success or ruin.'

The Athenians withdrew from the conference, and the Melians, left to themselves, reached a decision that was much the same as before, and gave this reply:

'Our decision, Athenians, is the same as it was at the first. We will not in a matter of moments give away the freedom of a city which has been inhabited for seven hundred years, but by trusting in the favour of the gods, which has preserved it until now, and in the assistance of men, that is, the Spartans, we will try to save ourselves. We ask that we be friends, enemies to neither side, and that you leave our country after making whatever treaty seems suitable to both sides.'

Such did the Melians respond: but the Athenians, just as they were leaving from the conference, said: 'Judging from your decision, it seems to us that you have the unique ability to see the future more clearly than what is sitting right before your eyes, and to consider what is out of sight as something that has already come to pass, simply because you wish it so. And what you have entrusted most in the Spartans — your fortune and hope— so also in these will you find yourselves most deceived.'[56]

It is only in an emergency that second thoughts emerge with any real urgency – and sometimes too late. The Mytilenian Debate took place and was resolved within the space of a day, because the Athenians only had that long to rectify their prior mistake and save the Mytilenians from annihilation. In the period following the June 2016 Brexit referendum, Theresa May spent years engaged in unpopular and unrealistic negotiations with the EU as Cassandra-like voices of warning piped up around her, unheeded. It was not until the eleventh hour — i.e. a few weeks before 29 March 2019, the original date fixed for Brexit — that anything started to happen. Suddenly, as disaster loomed too large to be ignored, Parliament mobilized, rebel MPs from the Conservative and Labour Parties broke away and formed their own, anti-Brexit party, and various demands for indicative votes, a second referendum and the repeal of Article 50 began to resound in the halls of power.

Fear sharpens the mind, but it does not always yield results – there was no breakthrough with a second referendum, no equivalent of the Athenians' faster trireme, and at the time this book went to press, most British people waited with a mixture of terror and relief for the Brexit promised for 31st October, 2019.

Lesson Four:
Widen the Net

The decree honouring the Samians for their loyalty to Athens and granting them Athenian citizenship, inscribed on a *stele* with relief showing Athena clasping hands with Hera.
(Acropolis Museum, Athens)

We throw open our city to the world, and never by alien acts exclude foreigners from any opportunity of learning or observing, although the eyes of an enemy may occasionally profit by our liberality.

PERICLES, 431 BC

On 26 May 2018, an anxious crowd gathered outside an apartment block in Paris. All necks craned upwards, watching as a young man scrambled up its façade, making his way as fast as he could to a toddler dangling precariously from a fourth-floor balcony. Many filmed the scene on their phones, not knowing whether the toddler would fall before he could be saved. Finally the man reached the balcony and whisked the child up by one arm, to collective relief. Footage of this extraordinary rescue went viral, and it was soon discovered that the man dubbed 'Le Spider Man' was in fact a twenty-two-year-old illegal immigrant from Mali called Mamoudou Gassama. News reached President Macron, who realized he must recognize Gassama's heroism in some way – but how?

Here was the perfect opportunity to make use of a national feel-good moment, at a time when public opinion was turning increasingly against immigration. Two days after the rescue, 'Le Spider Man' was welcomed into the Élysée Palace by Macron himself and given a medal, French citizenship and a job in the fire brigade, to make the best use of his talents. Gassama, who had also risked his life just a few months previously trying to cross the Mediterranean in a dinghy, leapt from *sans papiers* status to fully fledged citizen with one spectacular act of heroism.

This story divided opinion. Some (including the far-right politician Marine Le Pen) thought it heart-warming, and supported Macron's decision, while others derided the crassness of granting citizenship as a one-off reward. The questions surrounding immigration are quickly becoming the defining arguments of the twenty-first century: What do we owe 'outsiders'? Should rich foreigners be allowed to purchase passports? Should we give passports to poor but exceptional foreigners, like Gassama? Should citizenship be considered a privilege or a right? These issues are polarizing, because they cut to the heart of who we think we are.

Fears around immigration have shaped politics in both America and Europe in recent years, along with economic concerns. The Vote Leave campaign in the Brexit debate had two simple, winning promises: reclaiming £350 million a week from the EU, and stopping hypothetical Turkish immigrants pouring into Britain. Across Europe, concern over immigration ranges from unvoiced fears among voters to raging right-wing populism and neo-Nazism in generally liberal countries like the Netherlands, via the sitting governments of Austria and Hungary – and everything in between.

The Bulgarian political scientist Ivan Krastev describes those who are attracted to right-wing populism as 'the threatened majorities'.[57] Central and Eastern European electorates in particular are examples of 'majority groups that start to feel like persecuted minorities' – and that is increasingly true in Western European countries too.

Net immigration remained roughly the same in Britain for two years after the Brexit vote (a fall in EU immigrants matched by an increase in non-EU immigrants taking their place), yet concern over immigration in the UK dropped dramatically after the June 2016 referendum. In the days leading up to it, a poll showed that 56 per cent of British people named 'immigration and asylum' as the top issues facing the country. In October 2018, the figure was half that, just 27 per cent – and some other polls showed an even sharper drop over the two-year period. Why? Perhaps because Brexit quickly became such an enormous problem that it absorbed most other concerns, but more likely, alarmist immigration-focused headlines in the run-up to the referendum had simply put the issue foremost in people's minds. Once the headlines ebbed away, so did people's concerns; it is also likely that the referendum result acted as a form of catharsis, releasing pent-up anti-immigrant feeling.

In reality, concern over immigration is generally tied to rhetoric, not fact, and people who vote for anti-immigration policies often come from areas with low numbers of immigrants. In 229 of the 270 districts with a lower than average proportion of residents born outside the UK in 2011, the majority of people voted Leave, compared to only 44 per cent of people voting Leave in the seventy-eight districts with a higher than average population of foreign-born residents. In November 2016, only three of the sixteen American states that had an immigrant population of over 10 per cent voted for Trump. Paradoxically, citizens who have less exposure to immigrants can be those who fear them the most.

The ancient Athenians were hyperconscious of the sanctity of the citizen body, and jealously guarded citizenship to a self-destructive degree. In that, as in so many aspects of their society, there is a warning for our times. The Athenians had their equivalent Macron–Gassama moments, although for the most part they were less generous in bequeathing citizenship to others, and much more ruthless in taking it away.

Unsurprisingly, the Assembly generally voted in favour of attracting wealthy or useful people to Athens by offering certain privileges, much as Western democratic states do today. The possibility of becoming a Green Card holder is a dizzyingly exciting prospect for many non-American citizens who are more than prepared to be taxed without representation in return for the right to live and work in the US. Meanwhile in the European Union, there is a thriving market in Golden Visas in countries like Greece and Croatia, which offer residency and 'fast-tracked' citizenship to non-EU citizens who can afford to invest a substantial amount in the country, usually in property (in Greece, you receive a Golden Visa if you spend at least 250,000 euros, one of the cheapest schemes on the market, and particularly popular with Chinese investors who now own a significant share of the Athenian real estate market). Sometimes, for the right sum, you can get a passport without the tedious visa stage. In Cyprus, you can purchase a passport by making an investment of 2 million euros, and in Malta, a trifling 650,000 euros. In effect, these countries are competing, pricing themselves against each other, and the potential citizen is window-shopping when they look at the benefits offered in return for their investment by any particular country – it is a two-way investment.

Then as now, birthright trumped all else when it came to

full involvement in the democratic process in ancient Athens. Citizenship was restricted and withheld when politically convenient, like today, in ways which raise troubling questions in democratic societies with pretensions to egalitarianism. We can learn a lot from how the Athenians' misjudgements in excluding people they deemed 'outsiders' mirror our own – not just in how they can affect the quality of our democracies, but in their very survival.

The Democracy Club: Members, Non-members, 'No Entry' and VIPs

What would be your fantasy passport? And if you had to give up your existing passport to have it, would you?

Nowadays we think of citizenship primarily as a democratic right bestowed upon us at birth, regardless of our wealth, sex or ethnic background – this is, in many ways, one of the cornerstones of any self-respecting democracy. Most of the time, being born on a country's soil or with at least one citizen parent automatically confers citizenship. We can vote, we have a say in the future of 'our' country: we belong to it and it belongs to us – a deep, tribal relationship that we do not have to earn, although of course we have certain responsibilities as citizens. Citizenship is – again, theoretically – a right rather than a privilege, like the support of a parent. Yet the circumstances in which citizenship can be granted, removed or in some way diminished tell a different story.

In 2015, a fifteen-year-old British schoolgirl from London travelled to IS-held Syria and married a Dutch jihadi fighter. Four years later, two days after giving birth to a baby boy in a Kurdish-run refugee camp near her former IS home, she made an appeal to the British public to be allowed back to the UK.

Shamima Begum's story gripped the nation; in interviews, she said she regretted none of her actions and still believed in IS ideology, but wanted to raise her son in Britain, arguing she had done nothing wrong. Many people were unconvinced, arguing that she had, in effect, foregone her rights as a citizen by joining a group as antithetical to British values as ISIS, even if she had not committed terrorist acts herself. Some believed she deserved a second chance because she had been brainwashed as a child, and could be classed as a victim of human trafficking – and her child, also a British citizen, had certainly done nothing wrong. Sadly, he died a few weeks later, solving at least one problem for the British government.

Some who had little or no sympathy for her argued that Britain nonetheless had to fulfil its legal and moral obligations to a citizen, no matter what she had done. To sidestep this problem, the Home Secretary Sajid Javid stripped Begum of her citizenship. In doing so he arguably transgressed both domestic and international laws that protect an individual from being made stateless, claiming that she had the right to Bangladeshi citizenship and would therefore not be rendered stateless. (Bangladesh promptly vowed not to grant her citizenship, so this argument did not stand.) A couple of months later, Begum was granted legal aid to challenge the decision, and in a letter published by *The Times* her lawyer criticized Javid's decision as 'human fly-tipping'.[58]

The ancient Athenians would have approved in theory of Javid's course of action, but would have been concerned about the lack of due process. Withdrawal of citizenship (*atimia*) was the ancient punishment for serious crimes, including treason; it was no concern of the Athenians where those people belonged, after that, and modern legal concerns about statelessness would not have moved them. But at least they understood the importance of giving people like Begum a trial – and the importance of what that loss of citizenship would mean. There are some moving testimonies from Athenians faced with the prospect of losing their citizenship, such as Alcibiades the Younger (son of the infamous general Alcibiades), who in the early fourth century BC defended his dead father against charges of appropriating a racing chariot as his own:

Although the complaint involves money, the real issue is my right to continue to enjoy citizenship. For although the same penalties are prescribed for all by our laws, yet the legal risk is not the same for all; on the contrary, the wealthy risk a fine, but those who are in straitened circumstances, as is the case with me, are in danger of disfranchisement, and this is a misfortune greater, in my opinion, than exile; for it is a far more wretched fate to live among one's fellow citizens deprived of civic rights than to dwell an alien among foreigners.[59]

It is troubling that the attitude of Britain in the twenty-first century is even more extreme than that of the ancient Athenians – to deprive someone of their citizenship is to cast them out of society, arguably the most extreme punishment, short of the death penalty – and Britain is prepared to do so without trial to someone like Shamima Begum (who will be both deprived of civic rights and forced to live in exile, unless her appeal is successful). The withdrawing of citizenship was extremely rare in the UK before 2013, when immigration policies began to be tightened during Theresa May's time as Home Secretary, after she vowed to make the country 'a really hostile environment for illegal immigrants'.

More recently, under her terms as prime minister, the British government also made a habit of denying the existence of people's citizenship in the first place, as happened during the 2018 Windrush scandal, but of course Britain is not alone in this policy of forcing out long-established residents of disputed status, as Trump's America has amply demonstrated with its ramped-up ICE programme in recent years.

So much for being expelled from the democratic club – it is all too easy to join it. The practice of purchasing passports subverts the question of whether citizenship is a right rather than a privilege by rendering it a commodity. But the idea of earning citizenship by good deeds rather than wealth is an ancient one, as is the idea of attracting and profiting from desirable 'resident aliens' and rejecting undesirable immigrants – in other words, attracting investment *en masse* rather than from rich individuals.

The Athenian 80 per cent

At first glance, enfranchised Athenian citizens were a rarefied bunch – adult males over eighteen, comprising about 20 per cent of the population of Athens. The remaining 80 per cent were a motley group: foreigners who were resident aliens (known as metics), women, slaves and children. However, though the ratio of resident aliens to citizens in many democratic states today is much lower than in ancient Athens, they still form a significant proportion of the population. The classicist and political scientist Mogens Herman Hansen wrote in 1989 that 'modern democracies now have a *metic* problem, just like the ancient *demokratia*. "The whole of the people" no longer means the entire adult population, but the *citizens*, just as the term *demos* did in ancient Athens.'[60]

Oddly, before the mid fifth century, rules surrounding citizenship granted to foreigners had been more relaxed. A law attributed to Solon in the early sixth century BC made Athenian citizenship available to two specific categories of immigrants. In the words of the Greek biographer Plutarch:

He [Solon] permitted only those to be made citizens who were permanently exiled from their own country, or who removed to Athens with their entire families to exercise a professional skill. This he did, as we are told, not so much to drive away other foreigners, as to invite these particular ones to Athens with the full assurance of becoming citizens; he also thought that reliance could be placed both on those who had been forced to abandon their own country, and on those who had left it with a fixed purpose.[61]

Solon, like modern politicians, was clearly concerned with the question of the loyalty and talent of foreigners who were to be naturalized – it seems that he wanted to encourage these two particular kinds of immigrant, although he did not appear to care if their enthusiasm for Athens happened to be a matter of necessity, or some kind of aspirational admiration for the city. Solon wanted wholesale family commitment to Athens, recognizing perhaps that families that take root in a city and prepare for their younger generations to continue living there – by learning the language, building a social network – have more of an incentive to integrate than lone individuals who could easily move on.

His welcoming of 'those who removed to Athens with their entire families to ply a trade' is at odds with the policies of many affluent modern governments, which generally encourage solo adult immigrants to move temporarily to their country to work and send the money home to relatives, thus avoiding too much immigration while attracting cheap labour. The most notorious case of this is the Emirati countries, which attract Indian and Pakistani construction workers who exist in conditions of near-slavery, their passports confiscated until completion of work. Citizens of EU countries who migrate to work in more affluent

EU countries and send their wages home are also common, hence the casual racism towards the many Bulgarian domestic workers in Greece, or indeed towards Polish builders in the UK.

In Solon's welcoming of those who had been 'permanently exiled' from their own countries, he was, again, totally unlike modern governments who look upon foreign nationals who have experienced any kind of rejection in their home country with deep suspicion – the US, for example, does not permit any foreigner with a criminal record, or a history of institutionalized mental illness, to enter the country. Many countries do not even grant visas, let alone residency, to foreigners who cannot prove they have a certain amount of money in their bank account, plus a return ticket, to ensure they do not overstay their welcome. When countries do grant the right to remain to those who have nowhere else to go – political dissidents, or refugees of war or religious persecution – it is in the spirit of charity, albeit a charity enforced by international human rights laws and sometimes grudgingly given. Solon, far from seeing these people as charity cases, took the view that 'reliance could be placed on those who had been forced to abandon their own country' – he trusted those who had everything to gain by making a fresh start. It's a similar attitude that is often attributed to America as the land of opportunity, though some hopeful migrants have been tragically disillusioned.

Deserving Outsiders

It is unclear whether Solon's naturalized immigrants had full civic rights; what is more certain is that the descendants of these immigrants became Athenian citizens eighty-six years later with the tribal reforms of Cleisthenes, which is when he provided a legal base for naturalization. A large group of immigrants was incorporated into the citizen body under Cleisthenes, who divided up the entire population of Attica (the members of the four old tribes and all the other 'newcomers') into ten new tribes – meaning that for the majority of Athens' 'golden age', immigrants were very much included in the citizen body. According to Aristotle, 'Cleisthenes enrolled in his tribes many resident aliens who had been foreigners or slaves.'[62] The registration of an individual to a specific deme within a tribe became a prerequisite for Athenian citizenship, rather like today's electoral roll, although of course today you do not have to be registered to vote in order to be a citizen – yet another way in which modern citizenship is less demanding than it used to be.

Today, citizenship is sometimes granted to 'deserving' outsiders in the category of those in need: refugees or political exiles seeking asylum. Theoretically, in asylum cases the only relevant issue is whether the person has a 'well-founded fear of persecution' in their home country, but this is not always the case in practice. Western states are increasingly ready to admit that they prefer to accept Christian rather than Muslim refugees; it has long been an open secret among UNHCR camp staff, and some politicians – the Interior Minister of Cyprus Socrates Hasikos, Prime Minister Boyko Borissov of Bulgaria,[63] and President Viktor Orban of Hungary,[64] among others, have publicly confirmed their anti-Muslim refugee policy. The Slovakian government has gone so far as to breach EU law by refusing to take Muslim refugees at all.[65] It would seem that all 'deserving' refugees are equal in the eyes of the law, but some are more equal than others.

In Athens, as today, attitudes sometimes became less rather than more tolerant over time; this happened when the electorate grew, and when worsening economic conditions provoked resentment about 'outsiders', however fictional their numbers. Xenophobia does not have to be rooted in reality to flourish, or to be used for political ends. Trump's infamous 'Muslim ban' of 2017 banned citizens from a list of Muslim-majority countries from entering the United States, even if they had valid visas; the ban caused an outcry and was suspended, but now exists in a modified form (citizens of Libya, Yemen, Somalia and Syria are among those denied visas). Trump was responding primarily to the horror provoked among Americans by the growth of ISIS in Syria and Iraq and fears that Islamic extremists would flood the country. The number of Muslim immigrants admitted to the US since the height of the refugee crisis in 2015 has been a fraction of the number admitted to Europe – tens of thousands compared with millions, a pro-portional difference even more vast if the relative size of the

US (327.2 million people) is taken into account – and the existing checks on their entry into the country were some of the most draconian in existence. Better, in Trump's view, to ban all Syrians just in case. In Britain, the Windrush scandal was theoretically unrelated to the recent refugee crisis, but became affected by its aura nonetheless. Far more targeted anti-immigration measures have been brought into other European countries in the wake of the crisis, particularly in countries run by populists. In Hungary in 2018, Prime Minister Orban oversaw the introduction of a law which punishes lawyers and activists who give advice to asylum seekers with a year in prison – even donations of food were to be considered criminal.

In ancient Athens, by contrast, there was serious concern about an infiltration of foreign aristocrats.

Anti-Aristocratic Immigration Laws

Unexpectedly, Pericles the radical democrat, unparalleled champion of the masses, decided to clamp down on the existing criteria for citizenship. It is possible that – like many modern politicians – he wanted to be seen to be doing something to deal with public worries about the growing electorate, and fears of foreign influence in Athens. Before his reforms, Athenian citizens often married women from other city states, and their sons were called *metroxenoi*, meaning foreigners on their mother's side, and were also considered citizens. In 451/450 BC, an enactment was passed on Pericles' proposal restricting citizenship to persons of citizen birth on both sides – that is, you had to have both an Athenian father and an Athenian mother. It is a mark of the surprising and often cut-throat nature of Athenian politics that the man who enacted legislation granting the lower classes access to the political system and public office for the first time would make such a proposal, making the inclusion of foreigners in the Athenian citizen body by means of marriage impossible.

Politicians have always been notoriously prone to hypocrisy: Pericles is also the man who himself had an infamous relationship with Aspasia, an immigrant woman who came from Miletus to Athens, and with whom he had a child (and possibly married, though this is unclear). We know from Plutarch that Pericles persuaded the Athenians in 430 BC to have his son by Aspasia exempted from his own citizenship law, twenty years after it was passed, and to have the Athenian Assembly pass a decree in order to legitimize and naturalize him, because both his legitimate sons had died in the plague.

It is impossible to know exactly why Pericles restricted Athenian citizenship when he did, but it may have had something to do with stopping international aristocratic networks of influence. According to Aristotle's commentary on the Athenian Constitution, there were too many citizens in Athens at the time, but it is difficult to explain what this may have meant, especially since it is logical to assume that democratic statesmen in general are in favour of a strong *demos* and the more citizens, the stronger the *demos*. It is possible that they were the wrong *kind* of citizens – i.e. with the wrong loyalties.

After the Greek hostilities with Persia, which ended only in the middle of the fifth century, Pericles may well have considered it a priority to undermine the aristocratic loyalties of Athenian citizens to other aristocrats abroad, which were sustained by intermarriages, rather like European royalty. Even today, aristocrats and tycoons are often the subject of rumours speculating on their ties with other powerful people overseas. It may also have been the case that by Pericles' time there were many individuals who were acting as citizens without being citizens. There is no question that when the Athenian League was at its zenith, Athens attracted an impressive number of ambitious foreigners, like New York or London in their heyday.

Sometimes, wealthy foreigners misjudge the game of acquiring citizenship. In February 2019, Huang Xiangmo, a Chinese businessman, accused Australia of acting like a 'giant baby'[66] when his citizenship bid was cancelled due to suspicions over his political activities in China. This happened despite the generous donations he had already made to both major political parties in Australia – clearly, he had expected Australia to fulfil her side of the unofficial bargain. His story has some parallels to the British 'loans for lordships' scandal of 2006, in which it was revealed how significant donors to the Labour Party had been granted peerages in the House of Lords – not citizenship, of course, but access to the highest echelons of British power in return for cash.

During the entire classical period, i.e. throughout the fifth and fourth centuries BC, we know of only around 150 cases of naturalization, which was partly because foreigners resident in ancient Athens could not apply for citizenship, no matter how long they had lived in Athens or how much they might have contributed to the wellbeing of Athenian democracy and society as a whole. The only way to become an Athenian citizen if you were a foreigner was by being granted citizenship by means of an ad hoc, strictly defined legal process through a decree of the Council of Five Hundred and the Assembly. According to literary tradition there was a democratic law which established 'benefaction to the Athenian people' as the only criterion of eligibility for naturalization. Thus from Pericles' citizenship law onwards, the only ones who could become naturalized would be major benefactors – most of those were prominent foreigners such as rulers, wealthy individuals and politicians. They had no intention to live in Athens and make use of their citizenship rights and privileges, so in fact the naturalization act was primarily a form of reward in recognition of service to the Athenian people. The real purpose of this ultimate honour was of course to motivate other prominent individuals to emulate them – again, *plus ça change*.

Loyalty Rewarded

Towards the end of the Peloponnesian War, almost all of Athens' allies deserted her. Only one state remained loyal: Samos, an island close to modern-day Turkey. In an unprecedented move, Athens granted all the Samians Athenian citizenship in gratitude – about twenty-three years after they voted to kill all the Mytilenians to punish them for revolting. On closer inspection, however, the Samian decision may not have been gratitude so much as prudence: Samos was an important naval base in the Aegean for the Athenians in the final stages of the Peloponnesian War in 405/404 BC, and it was worth securing the Samians' ongoing loyalty, particularly at a moment of crisis. On their side, the Samians had long benefited from their alliance with Athens, and were terrified of being overrun by Lysander, commander of the Spartans; while risky, it was safer overall to stay on the Athenian side. Nevertheless, it was an extraordinary decision on the part of the Athenians, and fortunately the actual decrees involved in this act of collective naturalization have survived inscribed on a stone *stele*, decorated with a beautiful relief showing the two patron goddesses of Athens and Samos respectively (Athena and Hera) clasping hands in sign of friendship. This decree was set up on the Acropolis at the time of the grant of citizenship at the end of the fifth century BC (see the illustration at the beginning of this Lesson).

In ancient Athens, abolishing a decree required physical destruction of the stone *stele* on which it was written. The original stone *stele* showing the Samian decree was destroyed by the Thirty Tyrants along with many others, but after democracy was restored in Athens a few months later in 403 BC, it was recreated and a new one made, which we can see today in the Acropolis Museum. Here is the main text:

For the Samians who remained loyal
to the Athenian People

To praise the Samian envoys, both those who came previously and those who have come now, and their Council and their generals and the other Samians, because they are good men and eager to do what good they can, and the actions which they have performed are judged to have been performed rightly for the Athenians and the Samians, and in return for the good which they have done for the Athenians, and because they now attach importance to the Athenians and propose good things for them, the Council and the People shall decide: that the Samians shall be Athenians living under whatever constitution they wish.[67]

Mass enfranchisements on this scale were rare in ancient Athens, but another case which we know about from literary tradition, and which is also alluded to in Aristophanes' *The Frogs*, is the citizenship granted to all the men who manned the ships for the dramatic Arginusae campaign in 406/405 BC, the naval battle that took place in the last years of the Peloponnesian War. This was an act of desperation, in view of the urgent need to increase manpower, and also political expediency, much like the Samian enfranchisement.

The total number of men who manned the Athenian fleet for the Arginusae campaign in 406/405 BC was more than 20,000, of which maybe half were non-Athenian citizens: resident aliens (metics) and slaves. This act of mass enfranchisement was unprecedented in Athenian history since the time of Cleisthenes, when he included immigrants in the citizen body. After Arginusae, the fact that citizenship was granted not only to metics but also to slaves shows more than anything else the desperation of the Athenians to undertake the campaign and win the war. It vouchsafed the loyalty of these men and prevented them joining the other side, at a time when there was already a great shortage of men in Athens. This was also a unique occasion of granting citizenship without the prerequisite of being a benefactor of the Athenian state, and in that sense was made illegally. In other words it was likely expediency, rather than egalitarian ideology or even gratitude, that led to this massive enfranchisement in 406/405 BC.

While 'gifting' citizenship to foreign-born soldiers has its roots in the ancient world, it had its biggest renaissance in the twentieth century, particularly during the First World War. Immigrant soldiers comprised over 18 per cent of the US Army, many of them volunteering to serve 'to prove their loyalty to the US and demonstrate their patriotism for their new country', according to the US Citizenship and Immigration Services website – but in reality, most of the 500,000 who served were drafted. After the war, many of them were rewarded with citizenship – in 1919, 128,335 and in 1920, a further 51,972.[68] But times have changed. Under the Trump administration, many foreign-born recruits promised citizenship in return for signing up have been discharged because they have been deemed 'a threat to national security' under tightened immigration laws – the same rationale that lay behind banning citizens of Muslim-majority countries from US soil in 2017. In this, and in the mass enfranchisement of Arginusae, the granting of citizenship to foreign-born soldiers is first and foremost a political tool, deployed and withdrawn strategically.

A Temple of One's own

We don't know very much about the hopes and dreams of the vast majority of ordinary people living in Athens but occasionally we get a precious glimpse. We know, for example, that in the fourth century BC, a Cypriot woman called Aristoclea, far away from home, prayed desperately for something. She directed those prayers to 'celestial Aphrodite', the patron goddess of Cyprus, and dedicated something to the goddess – perhaps a statue, perhaps a pot – in the hope that it would make her wish come true.

We know this because we found her prayer inscribed on a block of stone, the base of her gift. It confirms the existence of a temple built for foreigners to worship their own gods as they pleased on Athenian soil. We know that in the fourth century, a decree was passed allowing the Kitians of Cyprus a plot of land in the port of Piraeus so that they could build their own sanctuary of Aphrodite. Bilingual funerary monuments of the Kitians, written in Phoenician and Greek, suggest that the 'Kitian merchants' were most likely wholly or partly of

Phoenician ethnicity (Phoenicia was in modern day Lebanon). Aristoclea's dedication shows that the sanctuary promised to the Kitians was duly built and operated.

This is the relevant text of the stone slab (*stele*) found in Piraeus:

> *Concerning what is deemed to have been the lawful supplication of the Kitian merchants who are asking the People for right of ownership of a plot of land on which to found a sanctuary of Aphrodite, the People shall decide: to grant the Kitian merchants right of ownership of a plot of land on which to found a sanctuary of Aphrodite, as the Egyptians have founded a sanctuary of Isis.*[69]

The 'lawful supplication of the Kitian merchants who are asking the People' was an important part of legal procedure in Athens. Supplication is an appeal to the mercy of another party – it is not exercising a right. The practice of having someone, either a citizen or a non-citizen of Athens, supplicate to the Assembly was a provision in the democratic practice in the fourth century BC, and there were several instances of supplication by non-citizens to the Athenian Assembly – in other words, they could exercise some civic rights despite not being able to vote.

The mention in the decree of another grant to the Egyptians to build a sanctuary of Isis (the equivalent of Demeter for the Greeks) suggests an interesting precedent for the decree for the Kitians. The relationship between Athens and Egypt was strong in the fourth century BC and the Athenians were keen to encourage Egyptian traders to visit Athens. Indeed, this facilitation of merchants must be seen in the wider context of Athens' efforts to improve its economy by allowing foreign merchants to worship their gods in their own sanctuaries when coming to the port of Piraeus. It must have been an incredibly vibrant and cosmopolitan place swarming with different people – a hub where 'outsiders' genuinely belonged, contributing to the economic and strategic power that Piraeus represented for Athens.

As of mid 2019, there is no functioning public mosque in Athens for the considerable Muslim community, most of whom are refugees who make do with unofficial rooms of worship in their own homes. The reason for this is a diplomatic feud; for decades, the Turkish and Greek governments have pursued a stubbornly reciprocal policy concerning the churches and mosques in their respective jurisdictions. The Turks refuse to allow the restoration of churches and monasteries on the islands off the coast of Istanbul, which were home to Greek Orthodox Christians during the Ottoman period, until a mosque is built for the Muslim population in Athens. While the Greeks have traditionally insisted that the restoration of the churches and monasteries must happen first, legislation has now been passed to build the mosque, but the project has been mired in bureaucratic delay. Ancient Athens did not have to deal with such annoying considerations when granting minorities the right to worship. Secure in its self-regard as a magnanimous superpower, the city state was free to be as radically open-minded and all-welcoming as it liked.

Insightful Barbarians

Early one morning, a boat docks on the coastline of Athens and a man, clearly not Greek, steps off hesitantly. He starts walking to the city centre – 'everything was strange to him, and many things made him feel uneasy; he did not know what to do with himself; he saw that everyone was laughing at his clothes; he could find no one to speak his native language.'

This was not a nameless refugee arriving in Athens in 2019, but a man from the early sixth century BC. Anacharsis was from Scythia (on the northern shores of the Black Sea), which was an area populated by migrants originally from eastern Persia. The description above of his vulnerability on arriving alone in Athens was written by his second-century AD biographer Lucian, also a foreigner. Lucian came to Athens from Samosata, on the modern-day Turkish–Syrian border, and his description of Anacharsis is characteristic of the intimidation felt by any human being who arrives alone in a foreign land with no knowledge of the local language or customs, and was probably inspired by Lucian's own feelings when he himself arrived. It continues:

In short he was completely sick of his travels, and made up his mind that he would just see Athens, and then retreat to his ship

without loss of time, get on board, and go back to the Bosphorus;
once there he did not have a long journey to complete before he
would be home again.[70]

Anacharsis did not leave, however; he became very close
friends with Solon, who at that time was consumed by his
legislation for Athens. When he became aware that Solon had
been appointed by the Athenian people to draw up a code of
laws, Anarchasis made the following, rather depressing, obser-
vation, felt if not articulated by people today reading headlines
about investigations into high-level corruption, collusion and
hush money: 'Laws are like a spider-web: it catches the little
flies but big ones pierce it.'

Anarcharsis was a classic example of the 'insightful barbarian'
with his outsider's eye (which is also generally recognized as
an asset in providing objectivity in everyday disputes, as in
third-party adjudication). 'Barbarians' was the original term
for the people of the Persian Empire; the word did not carry
the derogatory meaning that it acquired later, because in the
fifth century it meant primarily the other, the non-Greek – the
onomatopoeic 'barbar' evoked the incomprehensible language
these people spoke.

Anacharsis' friendship with Solon was significant. His
spider-web comment on Athenian legislation may well have
contributed to *isonomia* – equality in front of the law, one of
the major principles of fifth-century Athenian democracy. There
are plenty of modern examples of the invaluable 'outsider's eye',

particularly in the US: academics like Hannah Arendt, whose exile from Germany after the Second World War forced her to think deeply about the American society in which she found herself, and who contributed so much to Western political philosophy, or politicians like Madeleine Korbel Albright, born in Czechoslovakia, and later the first female Secretary of State in US history. Other contributors are less high-profile, but still have widespread influence; the foremost 'insightful barbarian' of Twitter, the London-based architect and satirist Karl Sharro (*@KarlreMarks*), has 140,000 followers and wields his Lebanese perspective to skewer European political culture: 'So three Arab commentators walk into a bar. They get funding from the EU and call it "A Panel Discussion on the Arab Spring". 8/05/12.'[71]

Anacharsis' biographer Lucian delivered his speech 'The Scythian' before the Assembly at Athens, speaking as a foreigner who also wished to be accepted by the Athenians. He therefore drew an analogy between himself and his more famous counterpart, and told his audience that Anacharsis received the privileges of Athenian citizenship, which suggests he was one of the first foreigners who was granted citizenship shortly after the concept was invented, but before Cleisthenes' reforms crystallized its rules. His naturalization shows how Athens was eager to incorporate wisdom into its citizen body, even from an outsider. Just as Athenian society had been open enough to appoint Solon as legislator to solve its problems in the early sixth century BC, so it was prepared to listen to a barbarian's constructive criticism.

Yet Anacharsis' story has a tragic ending. The historian Herodotus tells us that on his journey home to Scythia, he encountered a group of people worshipping the Mother of the Gods (a religion alien to his own people). The scene made an impression on him:

> *when he came to Scythia, he hid himself in the country called Woodland (which is beside the Race of Achilles, and overgrown with all kinds of trees); hidden there, Anacharsis celebrated the goddess's ritual with exactness, carrying a small drum and hanging icons on himself. Some Scythian observed him doing this and told the king, Saulius, who came to the place himself and seeing Anacharsis performing these rites, shot an arrow at him and killed him. And now the Scythians, if they are asked about Anacharsis, say they have no knowledge of him; this is because he left his country for Hellas and followed the customs of strangers.*[72]

It is sobering to think of instances in the modern world when this still happens – converts to minority religions who practise secretly before being found out and punished, never to be spoken of again, or political dissidents who have returned home to repressive regimes only to be imprisoned or killed on the grounds of having been 'corrupted' by foreign influence. Even more often, the punishment of those who 'followed the customs of strangers' can happen when Western culture pervades a society which has lopsidedly embraced it. In Kurdish and Turkish societies, the growth of social media has allowed online romances to blossom; the disruption this causes to the usual programme of arranged marriages can devastate families, causing lifelong rifts and in the worst cases, honour killings, which exist in a culture of silence. Cultural mixing, while a noble aim of liberal society, has the potential to make the individual a misfit in both societies, and in its worst cases, a marked woman or man.

Lysias the Orator

Everyone knew Lysias – he was the best public speaker in town, a prominent supporter of democracy, and a lawyer who usually won his cases. Born in Athens in around 445 BC, he had a wide circle of friends that included Plato and Socrates. His family also happened to be very rich, performing liturgies and even ransoming Athenian prisoners of war. But Lysias had enemies. Those who disliked him and envied his wealth liked to point out that his father had an accent, a whiff of Marlon Brando in *The Godfather* – a native of Syracuse, he had come to Athens on the invitation of Pericles before Lysias was born. Lysias himself was an *isoteles* – a metic who enjoyed added benefits such as the right to own a house and pay the same taxes as Athenian citizens, but was still denied the right to vote and to assume public office. Lysias discovered that in the wrong political climate, wealth and social status cannot get you citizenship – in fact, they can make life more dangerous.

Lysias was around forty years old when the Thirty Tyrants took power in Athens in 404 BC, a regime that was extremely aggressive to the resident aliens of Athens. The subsequent suffering of Lysias' family is evident in the speech he gave as an accuser of one of the Thirty named Eratosthenes.

And not even in respect of the smallest fraction of our property did we find any mercy at their hands but our wealth impelled them to act as injuriously towards us as others might from anger aroused by grievous wrongs. This was not the treatment that we deserved at the city's hands, when we had produced the choruses for all the dramatic performances that we were appointed at the festivals, and contributed to many extra-ordinary property taxes, when we showed ourselves men of orderly life, and performed every duty laid upon us; when we had made not a single enemy, but had ransomed many Athenians from the foe. Such was their reward to us for behaving as resident aliens far [better] than they did as citizens![73]

Lysias' family was subject to the Thirty Tyrants' targeting of wealthy metics, particularly those who supported democracy. The Tyrants carried out a purge which has recent historical parallels like the confiscation of the assets of wealthy minority communities such as the German Jews in the 1930s, although the primary motivation of the Tyrants was money, not race. Further back in history, a neater parallel is the Ottoman Empire, where Muslim subjects were generally poor but had legal and

social privileges over the richer Christian and Jewish subjects, who contributed much more to the economy, but were
taxed much more highly and given fewer rights – a two-tier
system existed like that of the citizens and metics in Athens.
It was politically opportune for the sultans to target wealthy
non-Muslims, just as it was politically opportune for the Thirty
Tyrants to target wealthy metics in Athens. However, the primary motivation in both cases was money – by 404 BC, when
the Tyrants took power, the Peloponnesian War had emptied
the Athenian coffers, just as the palace coffers were emptying
in the final decades of the Ottoman period.

Lysias' brother was executed by the Thirty Tyrants and he
himself had a narrow escape. He then played an active role
in the restoration of democracy which took place a little later
(in 403 BC) by offering his services to the democrats who
had been exiled by the victorious Spartans. The leader of this
group of democrats, Thrasyboulos, proposed a decree granting
citizenship to all foreigners who had been with him for the
restoration of democracy, but the proposal was blocked on a
technicality. It is obvious from Lysias' speech above that he was
not only indignant that his wealth and services to Athens had
not been recognized, but that he also craved a strong sense of
belonging to the Athenian *polis* which could be fulfilled only
by being given citizenship rights. It was never to be.

In the modern world, even when immigrants become
citizens they can often carry the stigma of being different
– perhaps even more so when they are well known and

powerful. George Soros, a Jew born in Hungary who came to the US in 1956 and built an enormous fortune from nothing, on the one hand embodies the American Dream, but the liberal, anti-nationalist agenda of his global political philanthropy has made him a target for many critics. Like Lysias, his wealth has contributed in large part to many people's dislike of him – 'our wealth impelled them to act as injuriously towards us as others might from anger aroused by grievous wrongs' – and his almost evangelical support for democracy, despite belonging to the privileged echelons of society, has been met with suspicion. Unlike Lysias, however, Soros, once a child refugee, benefited from America's great record of receiving and nurturing immigrants – a record that has seen better days than the present.

Consequences of Excluding Outsiders

The question of whether 'outsiders' deserve to be welcomed into the democratic clubs we have established for ourselves is a divisive one. The Athenians were a pragmatic lot; from them, we can see that however you define 'outsiders', if you want their contributions to society (in whatever form – economic, cultural, military) you need to give them access to political rights in order to reinforce a sense of belonging. Athens as well as other Greek city states never managed to become greater entities because of their inability to incorporate metics and other foreigners and enlarge the citizen body.

This was one important factor in the weakening of the Greek city state as a form of political organization in the late fourth century BC and its gradual demise during the Hellenistic and Roman periods.

Today, of course, we have more ethical considerations, and more complicated rules. We must ask 'who is deserving?' or indeed 'who has the right?' to citizenship – not just 'who do we want?' – because sometimes, even when individuals are legally deserving, we still don't want them, and find reasons not to include them. One of the most interesting illustrations of this is the Windrush scandal, which affected individuals from the Caribbean who were invited to come and live in Britain after the Second World War (the first group arrived on the ship HMT *Empire Windrush* in June 1948, hence the name). Some of them never made their British citizenship official, although as Commonwealth subjects they were entitled to it. In 2018, it was decided that if Windrush invitees, their children or grandchildren could not prove their citizenship in myriad ways, they could no longer access public services and were liable to be deported 'back' to the Caribbean. Few paid much attention to this until the *Guardian* newspaper started to publish the stories of people for whom even the highly immigrant-sceptic *Daily Mail* had sympathy: elderly Jamaican nurses who had worked for the NHS for decades and were now on the verge of deportation because they could not prove their status. Even then, the tabloids treated these nurses as though they deserved to remain in the UK because of their long years of service, their lack of criminal record or their consistent payment of taxes – not because they had the right, something that speaks of the systemic racism which still persists in the UK.

The British government has since apologized for its treatment of Windrush victims; the episode serves to show, however, that citizenship is often cast as a revocable privilege rather than a right. By contrast, the Athenians' treatment of individual citizens was at least clear-cut in a legal sense: as a citizen, you had freedom of movement, and your citizenship could not be queried or stripped from you unless you were convicted of a serious crime in a court of law.

Athens failed in a bigger sense because it excluded 'outsiders'; this contributed to its ultimate undoing, and the story of its fall serves as a very pertinent parallel to the existential debate currently surrounding the EU, and the US. Athens relied heavily on rich foreigners – metics, merchants and non-citizens who worked as moneylenders – and its economy was relatively healthy even after it lost its empire following defeat by the Spartans. However, there was a split between citizens (landowning but not predominantly entrepreneurial, and generally less well-off) and rich non-citizens. In some ways, this mirrored the split in the late Ottoman Empire between the poorer Muslim subjects and the richer Christian and Jewish subjects; the latter developed serious resentment as a result of their steadily worsening treatment as second-class citizens, and the empire became socially fractured, contributing in no small way to its eventual fall.

By failing to embrace other city states and not amalgamating itself into a stronger whole, Athens weakened to a point that became fatal when it was threatened in the late fourth century BC. Philip II of Macedon, father of Alexander the Great, accumulated enormous military strength by incorporating all the people he conquered into his army. This strength was then channelled into the Macedonian forces led by Alexander, and passed down to successors such as Antipater, the general who defeated Athenian forces and overthrew the Athenian constitution in 322 BC. This leaves us with a question: how big should a democratic state be to succeed? Too big, and it becomes impossible to maintain, overstretched and chaotic – and incapable of treating all its citizens (or subjects) fairly. Too small, and it becomes vulnerable, like Athens; the divide between citizens and non-citizens becomes obvious and breeds resentment.

There will always be outsiders, and the challenge for a democracy is how to incorporate them into society responsibly. Equal alliances have a habit of turning into hegemonies, and allies are rarely treated as well as citizens – as the next lesson shows.

Lesson Five:
Don't be a Superpower

Parthenon frieze showing a bull in the Panathenaic procession
being taken to the goddess Athena as an offering for sacrifice.
(Acropolis Museum, Athens)

Rule, Britannia! Britannia, rule the waves!
Britons never, never, never shall be slaves.
The nations not so blest as thee
Must, in their turn, to tyrants fall,
While thou shalt flourish great and free,
The dread and envy of them all.

JAMES THOMSON, AD 1763

With your navy as it is today there is no power on earth – not the King of Persia nor any people under the sun – which can stop you from sailing where you wish. This power of yours is something in an altogether different category from all the advantages of houses or cultivated land . . .

PERICLES, 431 BC

Democracy is incapable of empire.
CLEON, 427 BC

Sacrificial Cows

By the mid fifth century BC, Athens ruled the waves with the assurance of an early twentieth-century Britannia. She was not a monarchy, but acted like one, controlling a network of tax-paying 'allies' in the Aegean region within the firm grip of an unrivalled naval force. These allied Greek states, supposedly united on an equal footing with Athens in a defensive league against Persia known as the Delian League, were forced to send cows and suits of ceremonial armour to the birthplace of democracy, as well as more conventional taxes, as forms of tribute. If they tried to resist this arrangement or dared defect from the League, they were punished and democracy forced upon them in a way that strongly recalls the worst of twentieth-century imperialism.

Athens' treatment of her less powerful allies is obvious from literary sources, but the physical evidence – stark and unfiltered – is perhaps more shocking. The broken remains of a *stele* (stone decree) that stood on the Acropolis in the 420s BC, for example, shows us in pedantic detail the process of punishment imposed on any 'ally' who dared withhold the required tribute. Its partially complete text informs us that the same harsh penalties also applied to those who did not send a cow and ceremonial armour for the Great Panathenaea, the festival of Athena held every four years on the Acropolis, which originally had nothing to do with the allies, or protecting Greece from Persian forces. The *stele* suggests that some allies did indeed try to get away with not pledging cows for the goddess's pleasure, and were subsequently named and shamed – 'revealed to the Athenians', as the *stele* dramatically puts it, like criminals.

If any Athenian or ally does wrong concerning the tribute [phoros *– a word still used by modern Greeks for tax*] *. . . whoever wishes of the Athenians and the allies shall be permitted to write an accusation against him to the* prytany [*presiding committee of the Council of Five Hundred*]; *and let the* prytany *introduce into the Council the accusation . . . or they shall be penalized at their accounting for bribery* [*ten thousand?*] *drachmas each . . . When he is judged to be in the wrong, let the* prytany *formulate proposals about what he should suffer or pay. And if anyone does wrong with regard to the bringing of the cow and panoply, the accusations against him and the punishment shall be handled in the same manner.*[74]

A taste for domination does not spring from nowhere. Athens was already comfortable with controlling satellite states; since the eighth century BC it had been sending settlers to colonize lands abroad, as had other Greek city states. The cows and panoplies sent to Athens by allied states in the Delian League replicated the arrangements of Athenian colonists who sent the same gifts back to the metropolis for the Great Panathenaea (held every four years, unlike the Lesser Panathenaea that were held annually), as well as an enormous wooden phallus for the Dionysia, the festival of Dionysus (god of fertility and drinking) held in Athens in the spring. The contributions of allies to religious festivals entirely unconnected to them was a form of humiliation. Athena soon came to be not only the patron goddess of Athens itself, but of its empire; the sacrificial cow, and indeed the enormous phallus, might as well have been a token effigy of the subservient state itself.

Imagine the member states of NATO being forced to send turkeys, or phalluses, to the White House for Thanksgiving every four years. The sacrificial cow – immortalized on the marble frieze of the Parthenon as it is led to sacrificial slaughter – is the most obvious sign that the 'alliance' operated by the Athenians was in fact the hegemony of a single powerful nation over less powerful ones. It also helps us understand that perhaps this hegemony was inevitable, and inevitably exploitative.

League of Submissives

The Delian League of Athens and its allies started life as a military alliance in the spirit of NATO, composed of Greek city states mainly of the Aegean islands, and the coastal cities of Asia Minor (modern-day Turkey), just beyond the edge of the Persian Empire. It was set up in 478 BC, just after the end of the Persian Wars, and its mission was to defend its members from any future threat from the East (Persia). The initiative was taken by Athens, already the most powerful naval force in Greece after her victory against the Persians at the Battle of Salamis in 480 BC.

The NATO analogy is imperfect, but some parallels are worth noting: the North Atlantic Treaty Organization was set up as an alliance between the United States and European powers in 1949 to counter a threat from the East (Russia), and was dominated from the start by the US, just as Athens dominated the Delian League, even though in both cases the 'Eastern threat' was more pronounced for weaker states closer to danger (Western Europe, or the Greek city states closer to Persia). NATO has evolved from its original remit of guarding against Russia by becoming involved in conflicts in the Balkans and the Middle East, just as the Delian League evolved from its original remit of guarding against Persia to supporting Athenian interests against Sparta. Of course, NATO is still an alliance, while the Delian League came to be entirely monopolized by Athens for its own ends.

The League was 'Delian' because its treasury was first located on the tiny island of Delos in the middle of the Aegean Sea; the member cities contributed money to this treasury as a communal fund for the naval operations of the League. In 454 BC, after twenty-five years of controlling the money from the sidelines and making decisions on its expenditure, Athens took full and final control by moving the treasury from Delos to the Acropolis, at a time when the hawkish Pericles was dominating Athenian politics. Massive stone slabs, twice the size of a human being, were set up on the Acropolis listing the names of the allied city states and recording sums of money representing one-sixtieth of their overall tribute payments, which were given as a mandatory offering to the goddess Athena. In the first years of the League's existence, allied states had a choice of sending tax or triremes (warships) as their contribution. As time went on, however, they chose to pay tribute because they did not want to commit their ships to campaigns away from home, so Athens ended up collecting the League's money and using it for development of her own navy; as a consequence of this, she gained much more experience in naval operations than the allies.

The allied fleet and its operations were managed very efficiently by Athens, and the treasury coffers swelled: records show that the revenue from the allies amounted to approximately 500 talents, or 3 million drachmas (one drachma was the day's wage of a skilled labourer). The Athenians considered the surplus money as theirs, to be used for purposes not connected to the League's operations, such as jury payments, or the building of the Parthenon (which started in 447 BC).

So we come to the paradox of the democratic superpower: by the mid fifth century, Athens had become a radical democracy in the interior and a tyrant in her foreign policy towards her allies. Less than ten years after the League formed, the island of Naxos revolted and was forced back into submission by Athens. A few years later, the island of Thasos revolted, and was similarly repressed. This was a pattern that was repeated, and the Athenians ended up controlling a league of allies with an iron whip.

In 2016, the outgoing NATO Secretary-General, Anders Fogh Rasmussen, wrote in the preface to his book: 'The world needs a policeman. The only capable, reliable and desirable candidate for that position is the United States. We need determined American global leadership.' It was also in 2016 that Donald Trump was elected president, and fears that he would be the first American president to botch the traditional, if unofficial, job of leading NATO proved justified. At the summit in July 2018, he demanded that 'delinquent' allies should pay more than previously agreed,[75] having declared on Twitter two days earlier that 'NATO countries must pay MORE, the United States must pay LESS. Very Unfair!'[76] While Trump was correct in stating that America has long spent a higher proportion on defence than other allies, he overlooked the fact that the US has arguably made far greater use of its membership of NATO in cementing the country's global standing as a superpower. His demand that member states contribute 4 per cent of their GDP is reminiscent of the notorious reassessment decree dating from the 420s BC, which significantly raised the tribute paid by the Delian League's allies to around three times the level under Pericles. This rise came as a result of the demands of warmongering demagogues like Cleon; even non-members of the League were taxed, such as the island of Melos before its annihilation in 416 BC. (In response to Trump's more reasonable demand, NATO allies did indeed agree to raise their contributions by $100 billion over the following two years.)

Trump had insinuated that the US might be better 'going it alone' if other allies did not pay up. It is hard to imagine that happening – the US and NATO have been intertwined for better or worse since the latter's conception. Trump's presidency coinciding with the resurgence of a Russian threat, decades after the end of the Cold War and even longer after NATO was formed with a Russian threat in mind, has a certain poetic irony – doubly so, given that the alliance, and indeed the present world order, has been constructed relying on the stability of American power.

Forced Democracy

In 468 BC, the city of Phaslis, one of the principal commercial ports on the coast of Lycia (modern south-west Turkey) was freed from Persian rule against the wishes of its own citizens. The man responsible for this opportunistic act of forced liberation was the general Cimon, who subsequently forced Phaeslis to enrol in the Delian League and pay a hefty tribute to Athens equal to that provided by Ephesus — a major league member, according to Plutarch. In other words, under the fig leaf of democracy, Athens stole Phaeslis from Persia, becoming the world pioneer in imposing democratic governments on other countries already under its control, and in fighting proxy wars in other city states.

The previously mentioned broken *stele* which named and shamed underpaying allied states has been dated to the 420s BC, the height of radical Athenian democracy, imperialism and arrogance – the decade of the Mytilenian Debate and the peak of the political career of the demagogue Cleon, who won an unprecedented victory against the oligarchic Spartans on Pylos in 425 BC. This was the time when Athens was most under the influence of demagogues seeking to add to the empire during the Peloponnesian War, contrary to Pericles' advice.

We know from Thucydides that Pericles believed it was crucial for Athens to keep a firm hand over the allies of the League if Athens wanted to do well in the Peloponnesian War, but he was also aware of the immorality of this position. He equated empire with security, but also advised the Athenians not 'to extend the empire while the war is on, and not to undertake additional risks of your own making' – something that proved to be sound advice, which was ignored. He also acknowledged that a democracy turns into a tyranny when it becomes a superpower, incurring hatred from the people it controls. Yet he deemed this a price worth paying, a view which is common today among conservatives in the US, though usually couched in less direct terms:

> *It is right for you to defend what we all enjoy, the prestige the city gains by ruling [its empire], and it is right that you do not shirk the hardships or avoid seeking out glories: never consider this conflict about one issue alone, slavery instead of freedom, for it is also about the loss of your empire and danger from those whom you angered during your rule . . . Nor is abandoning our empire possible, even if there are some who in a moment of panic and political apathy want to play the morality card. For what you have now is basically a tyranny: you may not have been right to acquire it, but it is perilous for you to let it go.*[77]

Put in these terms, states under the control of a tyrannical superpower are like hostages – immorally taken, but impossible to free without repercussions. The only answer to this hostage situation is not to let them escape. In 446 BC, another important ally of Athens, the island of Euboea, revolted at a time when there was no Persian threat at all. Nevertheless, the revolt was deemed unacceptable and this time the general in charge of the operation to put it down and 'subjugate the whole of it' was Pericles himself. Here is a section of a *stele* that may date from Pericles' time but may also be from the 420s BC, that records the process of rehabilitating Chalkis, a city on Euboea, after its attempted revolt. It includes a creepy oath of allegiance and penalties for future transgressions, and reads rather like something a naughty child would be made to write out in detention:

The Chalkidians shall swear an oath in the following terms: 'I shall not revolt from the People of Athens by any means or device whatsoever, neither in word nor in deed, nor shall I obey anyone who does revolt; and if anyone revolts I shall denounce him to the Athenians, and I shall pay to the Athenians whatever tribute I persuade them to agree, and I shall be the best and fairest ally I am able to be and shall help and defend the Athenian People, in the event of anyone wronging the Athenian People, and I shall obey the Athenian People.'

All the Chalkidians of military age shall swear; and if anyone does not swear he is to be deprived of his civic rights and his property is to be made public and a tithe of it dedicated to Olympian Zeus. An embassy shall go from Athens to Chalkis with the commissioners for oaths and administer the oath in Chalkis and list those of the Chalkidians who have sworn.[78]

We have already seen an example of Athens imposing regime change on another state in the case of the Mytilenians (who narrowly escaped being exterminated — see Lesson Three); Thucydides describes a wholesale process of colonization of the island that dared to revolt against Athenian control:

Later, instead of imposing tribute on the Mytilenians, they divided the land, except Methymnae, into 3,000 allotments, 300 of which were set apart as sacred for the gods, and the rest they distributed to Athenian shareholders by lottery. With these shareholders the Lesbians agreed to pay a rent of two minae a year per allotment to work the land themselves. The Athenians also took over all the towns on the mainland that the Mytilenians ruled over, and for the future became subjects of Athens.[79]

Athens imposed a more democratic government on Erythrai, an Ionian city on the coast of modern Turkey, with its process set out in an incomplete *stele* (the gaps in the text are filled in with scholars' best guesses, below). This decree stipulates the exact way in which the people of that city should create a Council on the model of the Athenian one, but with 120 rather than 500 members, no doubt reflecting the smaller population size of the state:

There shall be a Council appointed by lot of a hundred and twenty men; A [man who is appointed shall be examined] in the Council, and . . . shall be possible to be a councillor if he is not less than thirty years old; [anyone rejected in the examination] shall be prosecuted. No one shall be a councillor twice within four years. The overseers and the garrison commander shall allot and install the Council for now, and in future the Council and the garrison commander shall do it, not less than thirty days before the Council's term of office ends. They shall

swear by Zeus and Apollo and Demeter, invoking ruin on one
who breaks the oath and his children; [the garrison commander
shall administer the oath].[80]

The existence of this decree proves that the Athenian electorate themselves voted to approve these terms – unlike the
unilateral decisions taken by most modern governments with
regards to foreign policy (it would be extremely unusual to
approve a decision to go to war via referendum, even – or
especially – when public opinion is strongly against it, as in
the case of the British invasion of Iraq in 2003). The irony of
a democratic power installing a democratic government in a
foreign state is always striking – for example, the parliamen-
tary system established in Afghanistan after the US invasion
of 2001 (ambitiously named 'Operation Enduring Freedom'),
which was undertaken in response to the 9/11 attacks and the
Taliban regime's sheltering of the al-Qaeda perpetrators. Foreign powers have interfered in civil wars throughout world
history, either straightforward power grabs masquerading
as support for local factions, or more long-sighted strategic
attempts to prevent a rival ideology establishing influence
(such as the support that America gave to the groups fighting
Russian-backed Communist fighters in Greece's civil war of
the 1950s, thus preventing Greece from becoming a Soviet
satellite state like many Balkan countries). More recently,
the war in Syria has become a chessboard of predominantly
Russian, Iranian, Turkish and American-backed factions.

Intervention can serve as a useful pretext for empire-building, or at least quasi-empire-building, for both democratic and non-democratic superpowers.

In all city states of the ancient Greek world, irrespective of whether they were members of the League or not, Athens supported the democratic parties. When there was civil strife, the democratic party of that city asked for help from the Athenians, whereas the oligarchic parties would seek the help of the Spartans; the flipside of the deal was that when Athens was deeply involved in the internal politics of another Greek city state it would impose a democratic constitution and regime to its own specifications.

Corcyra (modern Corfu) was an ally of Athens and copied her style of democratic government until 427 BC, when oligarchic factions supported by Corinth (an ally of Sparta in the war) tried to seize control of the island, arguing that the pro-Athenian democrats were 'enslaving Corcyra to Athens'. The fight that broke out between the pro-Athenian and pro-Corinthian factions led to an unutterably bloody civil war, in which 'fathers killed sons and sons killed fathers', the first of many throughout Greece. Thucydides tells us that the Athenians were partly responsible for exacerbating the situation by demanding loyalty from the democrats and rejecting the terms for an alliance proposed by the pro-Corinthian oligarchic factions. But equally, he paints the factions within Corcyra as self-interested power grabbers – all political idealism evaporated once the war got going. Both Athens and Sparta became involved militarily before leaving the Corcyrans to their fate, a pattern that was repeated throughout Greece in years to come.

> *While later, the whole Greek world, so to speak, was in turmoil, with rival parties in every state — populist leaders trying to bring in the Athenians, oligarchs trying to bring in the Spartans. In peacetime they had no pretext or willingness to invite them in, but in wartime when alliances were at hand for each to do harm to their enemies and bring their own advantage, these invitations were readily available for those wishing to effect a regime change.*[81]

The habituation of small states to the patronage – or even control – of a more powerful state is something still in evidence today, for example in the attitude of ex-Ottoman, Muslim-majority countries like Bosnia and Palestine to the money or political support of the modern Turkish government. Once, the Ottoman Sultan controlled these countries, and the extent to which its modern inhabitants embrace this legacy is evidence of how important power structures continue to hold long after any formal political yoke has lifted.

Superpowers Backfiring

Democratic superpowers have always been something of a contradiction in terms; power translates into domination, and there is an element of coerciveness in any empire which is fundamentally antithetical to democracy. Ambitious democratic states are like any other in that they are subject to hubris and eventual ruin. Lured by the dizzying possibility of world domination, the horizon stretching out before them, they act like heroes of Greek tragedy. As Pericles put it, in the words of Thucydides, 'With your navy as it is today there is no power on earth – not the King of Persia nor any people under the sun – which can stop you from sailing where you wish.'

Much like Britain or the US, Athens saw no contradiction in acting as a democratic power with despotic associations overseas. Athens' confidence in its moral superiority over those it ruled was based in its power, something that is also evident in the 'might is right' sentiment of 'Rule, Britannia!' This eighteenth-century poem, later an unofficial anthem, is about Britain's historic naval superiority, thanks to which it secured both its dominion over others and its safety from dominion by others ('The nations not so blest as thee / Must, in their turn, to tyrants fall') – seemingly a zero-sum game. Again, Pericles could be addressing early twentieth-century Brits with the advice he gave to his contemporaries – 'as long as you maintain your empire you have nothing to fear' (his qualifying advice – 'try not to add to the empire while you're at war' – was exactly what Athens did).

In the polarized classical world of the fifth century BC, Athens stood for democracy and Sparta for oligarchy, and during that time Athens had the money, resources and confidence to sustain both an empire and its own standing as a democratic superpower. In some ways, the situation between the Athenians and the Spartans was similar to that of America and the USSR in the Cold War – mutual mistrust, and an ideological battle between two opposing political systems, one of which was a democracy. The obvious difference is that the Peloponnesian War was anything but cold; at its end, the population of Athens was half what it had been before.

War desensitizes people to acts of cruelty and injustice, and three key moments of the Peloponnesian War illustrate this on the Athenian side. First, the Mytilenian Debate of 427 BC shows that the Athenians were, at that point (only four years into the war), capable of moral reflection and mercy. Eleven years later, however, with the obliteration of Melos, there was no regret. A year after Melos, the Athenians were arrogant enough to believe that they could successfully invade Sicily, despite the arguments of people like Nicias (and the prophetic advice of Pericles) to dissuade them. There is a case to be made that Athens' gradual propensity towards tyrannical treatment of others (both allied and enemy states) contributed both to the deterioration of its own democracy, and to its downfall as a state. The Macedonian domination of Athens in 322 BC was only possible because Athens had become too weakened, both politically and militarily, to resist it.

It would be nice to believe that democracy can thrive in good times and bad, but in truth failure undermines democratic societies. After its defeat in the Peloponnesian War against Sparta in 404 BC, and the brief but brutal eight-month regime of the Thirty Tyrants imposed by Sparta, Athens was weakened, and began to trust more in individuals to govern rather than relying on the *demos*. In short, Athens became afraid, and lost the radical democracy that had defined it in the first century of its existence. Conversely, democracy is often empowered by success – NATO being a case in point, although of course its democratic credentials have been doubted over the course of its existence.

There is a common expression in English and in modern Greek: 'You can't make an omelette without breaking eggs.' Looking at the history of superpowers from ancient times to the present day, there is an obvious assumption to make: that you cannot be powerful overseas without bullying your subjects (or allies) into submission, committing the odd war crime, the occasional transgression of democracy. Does it have to be this way – or is there another way to extend power overseas while remaining a true democracy? The likely answer is probably no, and ironically, the notorious demagogue Cleon said as much when he urged the Athenian Assembly to stay firm on their decision to massacre the male population of Mytilene in 427 BC.

> *Democracy is incapable of empire, and I am all the more convinced of this when I see how you are now changing your minds about the Mytilenians . . . What you do not realize is that your empire is a tyranny exercised over subjects who do not like it and who are always plotting against you; you will not make them obey you by injuring your own interests in order to do them a favour; your leadership depends on superior strength and not on their loyalty.*

Thucydides believed war and the quest for empire was inevitable. He noted a central battle of human nature – the rule of law (*nomos*) vs. the rule of nature (*physis*), and the problem of how we reconcile these two opposing forces in society. The classicist Peter Rhodes has made the point that Thucydides was clearly troubled about a certain paradox within himself: he was proud of the Athenian empire, but at the same time knew it did terrible things to others. How do you reconcile your egalitarian principles with your admiration for power? It is something that we still struggle with today, and is in fact a topic that is getting more and more divisive in recent years between those who argue that empire is indefensible, and those who argue that empire is great.

A vague imperial nostalgia was one of the sentiments evoked by Vote Leave's 'Take Back Control' slogan, an appeal to a time when Britannia ruled the waves and no one told her what to do. The presidents of Russia and Turkey style themselves as the Tsar and Sultan of reborn empires, unafraid to emulate the greatness of yore. In Putin's case, he has acted on this by annexing Crimea and invading Ukraine, while Erdoğan contents himself with an extensive programme of soft power in previously Ottoman subject states, particularly in the Balkans, and much fiery rhetoric against Turkey's ancient adversary, Greece, and evil Western powers in general. Trump's 'Make America Great Again' slogan, while not explicitly about empire, inspires a similar nostalgia for a bygone era of undisputed American glory. Appeals to lost empire, real or imagined, have proved spectacularly divisive among electorates across the board; the contemptuous attitude of the left towards those who feel pride in an imperial record enrages the latter, and the rift between the two camps becomes ever more entrenched.

The liberal view is that if we want to be true to democracy, we need to be committed to giving up empire, however painful that might be. Apologetic conservatives, especially American conservatives, argue that if the 'good guys' were to step back from their global hegemony, a void would be created which 'bad guys' would rush to fill – everyone would be worse off as a result, and moreover, liberals are hypocrites for knocking the privileges of world domination that keep them safe and prosperous.

It only remains to say that both Britannia and Athens no longer rule the waves; those empires are dead and buried. In Britannia's case at least, she is certainly no longer 'the dread and envy of them all'. The consequence of her mismanagement of an empire that at one point covered about the same surface area as the moon[82] seems to have finally caught up with her.

ACROPOLIS REDUX:
Ancient Democracy in a Digital Age

The potential of what the Internet is going to do to society
– good or bad – is unimaginable. I think we're actually on
the cusp of something exhilarating and terrifying.

—DAVID BOWIE, 1999

Imagine that, every week, referendum questions popped up on your phone screen: 'Inheritance Tax should be raised to 60 per cent: YES/NO. Tap the screen and press your thumbprint to securely register your vote.' Would you trust the process? Would it become annoying, empowering, addictive, banal? Would you begin to take it for granted, like a Facebook feed? If the questions suddenly stopped, would you feel robbed of a democratic right – even if you had rarely bothered to answer?

It is a strangely pleasing irony that twenty-first century technology is edging democracy back to its ancient roots.

Deliberative democracy is in vogue again, with a global trend towards citizens' assemblies to fix problems that elected representatives cannot seem to agree on; direct democracy is also back in the form of more frequent referendums, online petitions, and, arguably, magnified public opprobrium of governmental policy via social media. The Internet has ignited debate like never before, but it has also encouraged polarization. We are returning to – even surpassing – an ancient state of connectivity, although arguably we are also driven apart by the same technology that connects us. Decision-making is increasingly in the hands of the people in many democratic states from Ireland to India, but whether it can develop in a way that will be good for society in the long run remains to be seen.

Dystopian political satire is becoming uncomfortably plausible. Take Charlie Brooker's *Black Mirror* television series, for instance. The very first episode, which came out in 2011, features a British prime minister who has sex with a pig on national television at the behest of terrorist blackmailers, because a Twitter poll has indicated that his popularity ratings would drop if he refused. This was an extreme projection of the extent to which politicians increasingly 'perform' to win their target audience's approval, in calculated defiance of their critics (the most extreme case is of course reality TV star Donald Trump, and his wielding of incendiary rhetoric). Even more unsettling is another *Black Mirror* episode in which a contrarian cartoon bear named Waldo runs for parliament, his popularity soaring as he slanders his rival candidates from established political parties. As his foul-mouthed jokes become ever more extreme, the guilt-stricken actor who voices him has a crisis of conscience and implores the public not to vote for Waldo, to no effect.

The idea of a joke-gone-wrong evokes not only the buffoonery of Trump and Boris Johnson but more literally the comedian Jimmy Morales, who won the presidency in Guatemala in 2015 with 67.4 per cent of the vote, the comedian Beppe Grillo, who in 2009 co-founded Italy's Five Star Movement (the party which went on to win the highest number of votes in the 2018 general election), and the comedian Volodymyr Zelensky, who played the president on local Ukrainian television and ended up winning the actual presidency in the 2019 elections. Perhaps pundits should have been less surprised by these results; comedians entertain, they are relatable, human, non-stuffy, popular by nature. The election of these seemingly absurd non-candidates has been a rejection of traditional democracy, and should serve to show the extent to which entertainment is increasingly intertwined with the business of government.

The future of democracy can look bleak, but there have been, as previously discussed in the cases of Switzerland and Ireland, some more promising developments in recent years – ancient Athens is flickering back to life in far-flung democratic states across the world. Here are a few more examples.

Return of the Council of Five Hundred

Iceland

The tiny republic of Iceland was hit disproportionately hard by the 2008 global financial crisis. Three big Icelandic banks came tumbling down, inflation and unemployment soared, people lost their houses and jobs. There was a real crisis, which had one positive outcome: the Icelandic people began to scrutinize power in a way they had never done before.

It was a 'constitutional moment', according to Erikur Bergmann, a burly Icelandic academic in his early fifties, addressing an assembled crowd of political scientists in Athens eight years after this moment of scrutiny. 'What the Icelandic people found was an unsustainable capitalist system.' According to Bergmann, Iceland's constitutional crisis should be put more broadly in the context of three major crises of the past century – the 1972 oil crisis, the 1989 collapse of communism and of course the 2008 financial crisis. Waves of right-wing populism followed in the wake of all three crises, which, as Bergmann argues it, led inevitably to the erosion of liberal democracy. He thinks the good news is that crises like this can ultimately result in an opportunity for democratic societies to examine what has gone so badly wrong and how to fix it.

The advantage of Iceland having a tiny but motivated electorate (there was a turnout of 75 per cent at the presidential election of 2016, of a population of 340,000) was that they could take decisive and rapid steps to rectify this 'unsustainable' system. Iceland's parliament, the Althing, is the oldest in the world, dating from AD 930. In 2011, it approved the most ambitious modern experiment in deliberative democracy: the crowdsourcing of a new constitution by the people themselves.

The Icelandic project was – from a certain perspective – deeply Athenian. First, in October 2010, a thousand people were chosen randomly from the electoral registry (electronically, rather than with a stone *kleroterion)* to reflect the make-up of the population as a whole. The modern process of 'stratified sampling' – which ensures that different segments of the population are proportionately represented (men and women of different ages, and from different parts of the country) – is essentially a more progressive version of the sampling of tribe members that Cleisthenes introduced in his reforms of 508 BC. The thousand randomly chosen Icelanders formed a 'constitutional assembly' which gathered and deliberated for a single day, discussing how to improve the existing constitution dating from Iceland's independence from Denmark in 1944 (it had been modelled almost exactly on the Danish constitution, with references to 'the king' replaced by 'the president'). The council decided the constitution should be rewritten almost from scratch – suddenly, the role of the great sixth-century BC lawmaker Solon was in the hands of the twenty-first-century Icelandic public.

The story then gets even more Athenian – an obsession with fairness and strict electoral procedure took centre stage. According to an EU progress report released in October 2011,[1] 'the elections for an advisory constitutional assembly held in November 2010 were annulled in January 2011 by the Supreme Court, due to flaws mainly relating to *insufficient secrecy of the ballot*' – this turned out to be an essentially meaningless discrepancy of around 15cm in the height of the ballot box from the standard Icelandic level. The fates of the twenty-five newly elected representatives of the advisory assembly – among them doctors, priests, professors, a farmer, a disabled rights activist, a nurse, a philosopher and a theatre director – looked uncertain, but the Althing stepped in by reappointing them as a Constitutional Council rather than an assembly, and told them to get to work.

Just like the Council of Five Hundred in ancient Athens, the new council's job was to make proposals which would then be either accepted or rejected in a national referendum (as the Council of Five Hundred's proposals would have to survive a vote on the Pnyx). Their process of deliberation turned into a remarkably broad, open conversation with the Icelandic public conducted over the Internet; the twenty-five members livestreamed their meetings on Facebook, inviting comments and suggestions, and posting on YouTube and Twitter in a flurry of interactive debate. The extremely serious business of deciding on, among other things, 'the division of powers between legislative and executive, the independence of the judiciary, environmental issues including the ownership of and the right to harness natural resources, the status of the State church and the delegation of powers by the State to international organizations' were decided in the course of four months in a nationwide debate conducted over social media.

It must have been a daunting but engrossing process. Imagine the prospect of contributing directly to your country's brand-new constitution; the kind of throwaway comments and self-consciously humorous opinions we write on social media on a daily basis would suddenly have to mean something, to be constructive rather than critical, to be responsive and carefully considered rather than cavalier and opinionated. Those in the twenty-five-member council would have felt enormous honour but also an overwhelming responsibility to express both their own opinions and those they had listened to – the same emotions that Athenian members of the Council of Five Hundred would have felt so many years ago.

There was huge public excitement when the council decided unanimously on the final version of the constitution; even more so when nearly two-thirds of the population voted to implement it in the nationwide referendum that followed in October 2012. A brave new era, a fresh start, a democratic blueprint designed *by* the people, *for* the people!

It never came to pass.

By the time the reform bill was brought to parliament, the 2013 Icelandic election had been won by opponents to the new constitution, and the bill has been stuck in limbo, unratified, ever since. A failed experiment in deliberative democracy, it nevertheless shows us what is possible – and other countries are taking note.

Australia, Brazil, Taiwan

The Icelandic crowdsourced constitution has been the most dramatic – and in some ways tragic – recent experiment in a gradual trend towards deliberative, or participatory, democracy. Over twenty years ago, the 1998 Australian Constitution Convention was gathered to decide whether or not to retain the Queen as head of state. One hundred and fifty-two delegates were chosen to consider making Australia a republic rather than a constitutional monarchy, but unlike Iceland, these delegates were not selected via stratified sampling from the electoral roll – half were elected by voluntary postal vote (voting is usually mandatory in Australia), half appointed by federal government. A majority of the Convention voted in favour of a new republic, but the public then voted that proposal down by 54.87 per cent to 45.13 per cent, preferring to keep the Queen. This result supports the theory that the mood of the *demos* is often more instinctively conservative than that of elected individuals – if there is a generally happy status quo, there is no move for change. By contrast, the post-austerity, anti-immigration mood of Britain led to the reactionary Brexit vote in 2016.

A game-changing democratic innovation from the last century was participatory budgeting, which started in Porto Alegre, Brazil in 1989 as an informal way for neighbours to get together and decide on how the municipal budget should be spent on things that mattered to them. This is now known as the Porto Alegre model and has been adopted by governments and businesses across the world, allowing citizens and consumers to sign off on spending plans. At the end of the twentieth century, the Internet was only just taking off, and there was less scope for building consensus among huge numbers of the public. A digitalized version of the Porto Alegre model emerged in 2012 in the form of an initiative in Taiwan. Like Iceland, Taiwan is uniquely well-suited to experiments in deliberative democracy, but for rather different reasons. While only a third of the size of Iceland, it has a population of 23 million (compared to Iceland's 340,000), a huge proportion of whom use the Internet. The island only became a democracy in 1987, following a history of occupation and military dictatorship, and held its first direct presidential election in 1996, so Taiwanese democracy is still arguably in its formative stages – and citizens want a say on everything, from budget spending to alcohol licensing.

In 2012, a group of civic-minded Taiwanese computer programmers took it upon themselves to build a system which invited citizens to audit Taiwan's central government budget – this grew into the '*gØv*' ('gov-zero') citizen community that was embraced by Taiwan's government and is now being emulated in countries like Italy and New Zealand for local government. Of course, online initiatives are arguably undemocratic in that they exclude offline members of the electorate (particularly the elderly demographic) – they are not entirely representative of the population, and they are certainly not randomly composed groups of decision-makers. But they do seem to 'get the job done', as politicians are fond of saying. Other, more practical problems in Taiwan, like how to ensure children do not buy alcohol with the advent of online alcohol licences in 2016, have been solved by an initiative known as *vTaiwan*, which connects members of the public in an online community and allows them to come up with a list of recommendations which are then submitted to the Taiwanese government, who can choose whether or not to implement them. This last point is, of course, key – if a government is not committed to implementing the decisions of a citizen body, it can look at best like the democratic equivalent of a patronizing pat on the head and at worst like a miscarriage of democratic justice, as Leavers in the UK have claimed in the face of opposition to implementing Brexit post-2016 referendum.

Turkey

While Turkey has the trappings of a democracy, over the past decade it has often failed to function as one, dominated by one-man rule and his grip on the media, the legal system and the economy. Ironically, this situation has also given rise to some impressive displays of civic unity, for example the extraordinary and moving spectacle of volunteer election monitors sleeping with their arms round ballot boxes, as mentioned earlier. The goal of the protective monitors was to ensure the boxes would not be stolen and their contents replaced by pre-stamped fraudulent ballots in the hours between the polling stations closing and the boxes being handed over to the electoral board. This happened in the 2014 local elections, and again in the 2019 local elections, and the results of both were contested by the losing side. In the case of the 2019 election for Istanbul mayor, which was unexpectedly won by the opposition candidate Ekrem Imamoğlu, President Erdoğan called for a re-run, accusing him of 'stealing' victory. To everyone's surprise, Imamoğlu won again two months later, by an even greater margin – proof that intimidation can sometimes backfire, and cause for hope that determination can bring about change.

In a country where democracy is so obviously threatened, people have to rise to the occasion of protecting what little democracy is left, just as the Athenians of the fifth century BC, understood that they had to protect their freshly minted democracy or regress to the tyrannies that came before. During the Gezi Park protests of June 2013, when riot police clashed with anti-government protesters in cities across Turkey, there was a period of two weeks when there was no police presence whatsoever in Taksim Square in Istanbul, where the protests had originated next to Gezi Park. This was an opportunity for serious anarchy to take root, but instead, the hive mind of the protesters took over and they began self-policing. Their predominantly peaceful mood meant that during those two weeks the square was safer, cleaner and friendlier than in living memory – protesters organized human chains of water bottle distribution, everyone cooperated to collect rubbish, there were free medical tents and spontaneous musical performances. This happened, in retrospect, because there was a common purpose that united all those present in the square, a sense of optimism and an instinctive understanding that everyone mattered – it was the antithesis of 'every man for himself'. If food had run out, it might have been a different story, of course, but until the police stormed the square, those two weeks were a brief and unforgettable utopia.

In a country of one-man rule, measures officially designed to open up power to the people are suspect, to put it mildly. In early 2014, as part of the ruling Justice and Development Party (AKP)'s Peace Process – an attempt of vacillating sincerity to solve the decades-long conflict with the PKK, a Kurdish separatist group in the south-east of the country – the government announced that it would be setting up a council of 'wise men' to travel the country, discussing possible solutions with members of the public and presenting their findings to the government at the end of it.

On 4 April, a few weeks after the plan was first announced, the government published a list of around sixty members it had appointed. There was no random selection from the electoral registry here: these were overwhelmingly male, pro-government celebrities and journalists. Unlike Iceland's and Ireland's citizens' assemblies, their meetings were closed and their recommendations to the government were also private. It is highly unlikely that this group of 'wise men' would have solved the decades-long Kurdish conflict, but we will never know, because in the summer of 2013 the dormant conflict between Turkish troops and the PKK reignited, and the much heralded Peace Process became a thing of the past.

Return to the Pnyx

In the introduction to this book, we suggested that the idea of replicating an ancient Athenian style of direct democracy via the Internet might not be a great idea in the age of mass targeted disinformation. Public ignorance, conspiracy theories and government propaganda have always been around, but the difference today is the Internet's capacity for targeting specific groups of people with 'alternative facts' designed to appeal to them, to an extent that was not possible before. The Internet should theoretically allow people to be more informed – the click of a button throws up information that would previously have taken much more time and energy to find out – but that assumes people want to be more informed. In fact, they tend to look for confirmation of what they already believe, and want to continue to believe. Another digital blow to democracy is the potential for electoral fraud, which is magnified to a hideous degree when voting is digitalized. As Tom Stoppard put it in his 1972 play *Jumpers*, 'It's not the voting that's democracy; it's the counting.' Both these problems make the idea of enabling direct democracy at the level that the ancient Athenians experienced problematic, although these problems could theoretically be solved.

Operating direct democracy via technology is not a new concept. Before the Internet had taken off, in 1988, the Danish academic Mogens Herman Hansen discussed the idea of 'televoting' – i.e. voting by interacting with a television set. Earlier still, in 1953, Ray Bradbury's dystopian novel *Fahrenheit 451* imagined a similar interaction, with viewers contributing – or believing they are contributing – to the plots of TV dramas (an idea that is, incidentally, now being introduced by the streaming giant Netflix with shows like *Bandersnatch*). For some years now, talent shows like *The X Factor*, *Strictly Come Dancing* and *Britain's Got Talent* have operated a voting system whereby viewers can text or enter online a vote for their favourite performance of the night, something that inevitably makes people feel more invested in the programme. Viewing figures for the finales of this kind of talent show are generally rivalled only by major sporting events – sport being the other great exercise in individuals' sense of investment in the performance of others.

Direct democracy in the true political sense, rather than in the realm of entertainment, is not to be taken lightly. Today we have checks and balances in our democracies in the form of institutions that the Athenians didn't have – they had penal measures which were far too harsh for our modern societies to stomach. Arguably, our institutions are actually stronger than their Athenian equivalents, and we do not allow the same concentration of power, which is ultimately a good thing. Direct democracy is a huge concentration of power in the hands of the people – which is why its digitalization and proliferation without necessary checks could be so problematic.

India and Indonesia

India is the biggest democracy in the world, with a population of over 1.3 billion and an electorate of 900 million people – an eighth of the world's population. How do you go about governing that number of people with a centralized, democratic government? India is about as far from the ancient Athenian-sized model state as possible, riven by many more divisive factors, prone to the modern malaise of nationalism and a logistical nightmare to run – elections happen only every five years because they are such an enormous undertaking. Yet unlike many other countries which became independent after colonial rule, it has never descended into military dictatorship or civil war since achieving independence in 1947.

India is one of those countries 'in name a democracy [but] in fact the rule of the principal man', as Thucydides said of Pericles in ancient Athens. Narendra Modi, a Hindu nationalist, has been in power since 2014 and is not above stoking the deep Hindu–Muslim fault lines of the country while boasting about his 56-inch chest. In April 2019, general elections began – the country is so huge that they last six weeks – and, as with many polarized countries today with populists at the helm, it was effectively a referendum on Modi himself, who won resoundingly.

India has never actually held a national referendum; in 1967, a local referendum was held in Goa to determine its future as a union territory, but in general, direct democracy has not been a feature of the country's political landscape. That might now be changing, at least at a local level – which is probably the way forward for such a big country. As with Taiwan, alcohol licensing law has been one of the most galvanizing issues for local communities, because it is one which has the capacity to affect people very directly. In January 2018, the residents of Tilak Nagar in western New Delhi voted in a highly unusual local referendum on whether or not to close down a local liquor store – nearly two-thirds voted in favour, and the result was considered binding: cue (dry) jubilation. In 2015, women in the northern state of Bihar, fed up with their alcoholic husbands, petitioned the state's chief minister Nitish Kumar to do something about it; he won the local election on the promise that he would ban the sale and drinking of alcohol entirely, which he proceeded to do. (Crime began to fall shortly afterwards.)

Indonesia shares India's problem of a vast electorate – 193 million voters – which has had tragic results. In April 2019, the presidential, national and regional elections were all combined on one day with the objective of saving money; 80 per cent of the electorate turned up at more than 800,000 polling stations, and around 7 million people were employed to count the ballots by hand. The effort was unprecedented, and so were the consequences: 272 ballot counters died from fatigue-related illness in the day that followed, and 1,878 of their colleagues fell ill. As populations rise, countries with hundreds of millions of voters will have to reform electoral procedure, either by simply spending more on it or by digitalizing the process – and it is much more likely the latter will win out.

THE OWL OF ATHENA

The birthplace of democracy is going through a tricky time. Over the last decade, nationalist parties in Greece have become emboldened by turmoil in neighbouring regions, even more than most European countries given its position on the edge of the continent. In May 2012, Golden Dawn entered parliament for the first time with 7 per cent of the vote, riding a wave of support which owed much to growing resentment at the nascent refugee crisis, as well as economic gloom. The party's website, along with those of supremacist groups and blogs, promotes the idea of Greece's superior ethnic pedigree by appropriating the texts of ancient writers like Thucydides. Who, in their eyes, immortalized wars between the ancient Athenians and their inferiors. Herodotus, who wrote about the invasion of Greece by 'barbarian' Persians, is a particular favourite among anti-immigration activists. To the Golden Dawn mind, modern refugees are the equivalent of Persians or eastern infidels trying to invade Greece in boats crossing the Aegean.

In response, the far-left Syriza government sought to down-play the classics during its 2015–2019 term by replacing them with more 'inclusive' subjects in schools. In 2016, the Minister for Education announced that certain ancient texts would be removed from the high school curriculum, including famous passages of Thucydides and Herodotus, on the grounds that such texts promoted the idea of empire and excluded immigrant children in schools. After a public outcry and formal complaints from academic unions, the ban was overturned in 2017, but the government's anti-classics agenda continued: in 2018, the Education Ministry announced that Latin would be replaced by sociology in high schools by June 2020.

These bans were a sign of a still-unfolding battle between left and right in Greece – one in which ancient texts have been weaponized, and in which Greek educational bodies have assumed the role of referee, stepping in to defend the classics while acknowledging the danger of their misuse at the hands of ultranationalists. In response to the 2018 ban on Latin, the Philosophy School of the University of Athens pointed out that banning classical texts, Greek or Latin, could prove counterproductive by confirming the 'one-sided admiration' by conservatives for ancient writers, 'with all the unpleasant consequences this may have'. Pericles' Funeral Oration, quoted on the Golden Dawn website,[1] was singled out for elimination by the Greek Minister of Education in 2016 and subsequently defended as 'essential' reading for children by the Society of Greek Philologists. Blow by blow, text by text, the tussle has continued to play out under the government of the right-wing New Democracy party.

Conservative readings of Thucydides' work have not been confined to Greece. In 2017, Republican hawks in the US became fixated by the Thucydides Trap, a theory proposed years earlier by the political scientist and White House adviser Graham Allison. The theory paints China as a new power challenging an established power (the US), just as the rise of Athens in the fifth century BC threatened the more established power of Sparta – in both cases, Allison argues, war is the only logical conclusion to untenable rivalry. Allison's work has been much derided by ancient historians and modern political scientists alike but has captured the imagination of, among others, President Xi of China himself, who told a group of Western visitors to Beijing in 2013 that 'we must all work together to avoid Thucydides' trap'.[2]

Academics have long pointed out that Thucydides frustrates simple interpretations, but we are not living in an age of nuance, and his work remains obscure. It is unsurprising that right-wing politicians have been able to reduce his texts to belligerent sound bites without being challenged. With a lack of real understanding and context has come an almost religious reverence for the so-called father of military history, and very little scrutiny of the interpretation of whoever can quote (or misquote) his work; Greek politicians' invocations of ancient writers are comparable to American politicians' invocations of the Bible. As one American academic described it, off-record: 'In the States, when appeals are made to the Bible at least half of the country groans. In Greece they all seem to buy it – except the far left.'

The weaponizing of history by politicians is one of the reasons we thought it important to write this book. The opportunistic appropriation of ancient texts is just one way in which the modern world is becoming enmeshed with history in bizarre and sinister ways, helped along by the Internet – which has fully borne out David Bowie's prediction to be both 'exhilarating and terrifying'. It connects people to a degree not seen since ancient times, but it also facilitates demagoguery and the spread of dangerous misinformation, as well as supporting people's natural tendency to polarize and form gangs. Technology is now on the cusp of bringing power to the people in radical new ways, and that comes with daunting responsibilities and dangers. Reintroducing some of the original tenets of democracy as digitalized democracy takes off might be one way of not only mitigating the negative effects of the Internet, but actually creating a new form of democracy for our times.

While writing this book we tried, semi-jokingly, to come up with ideas for how we could solve current crises by adopting Athenian principles. The most obvious problem of our time is vast, uninformed electorates; is it really acceptable to allow people to vote if they have no idea at all about what they are voting on? One of our more hardcore ideas included testing people to check they had read, or watched, the basic facts and figures and main opposing arguments of a question being put to vote – just as Athenian citizens were forced to attend the debates held on the Pnyx before a vote, and like the participants of the citizens' assembly in Ireland in 2016 had to read information packs and listen to opposing activists before coming to their conclusions.

This idea has overwhelming downsides: for one thing, it might dramatically reduce the number of eligible voters, a very undemocratic outcome. But it also has a despotic feel to it. Is the situation really so bad that we have to examine the entire electorate, separating the informed from the uninformed, violating a central principle of democracy that everyone should have an equal voice? Which of us knows everything there is to know about every referendum question, anyway? At its worst, the idea of the enforced education of voters brings to mind the chilling policies of the fictional populist Vivienne Rook in the dystopian 2019 BBC drama *Years and Years*, who calls for IQ tests to determine which citizens should be allowed to vote.

More practically, how would people prepare for these tests? The Swiss government sends information packs through voters' letter boxes ahead of referendums, but is it healthy to get everyone to read the same thing? Ideally, people should be informed from different sources, like a cross-pollinated ecosystem. Whatever happened to the time-honoured notion of the unmonitored wisdom of the crowd – do we have so little trust in people's common sense?

Even if governments were to send information packs to voters like the Swiss – which would, on balance, probably do more good than harm – there is something more important missing from modern societies: genuine interest in how the country is run. The more citizens are required to do (and they are currently required to do very little), the more they are forced to be engaged. What if democracy was more like jury service? What if modern-day citizens were called upon to assume public office as the ancient Athenians were? The huge electorates of today would result in a much smaller likelihood of actually being picked than was the case for ancient Athenian citizens, but even the possibility of performing a public service at some point would make us feel more interested in government, and in how we could help shape the direction of our country. As it is, a worrying proportion of modern electorates have never voted, have no intention of voting and might go to their graves without knowing or caring who their local representative was – and we do not entirely blame them, such is the depressing nature of politics worldwide. If you were picked to serve on your local council, or even in your national parliament, you would be committed to understanding the process of solving at least some of the problems faced by the rest of the electorate. It would not be an option to be disengaged.

Human beings instinctively seek engagement and kinship, the positive side of a tendency to form gangs – that is why we join clubs, religions, political parties, even protest movements. Political allegiance can come to feel like religion, in that it gives meaning to our lives. Cleisthenes understood the need to create tribes of people who would feel connected merely because they were told they were – kinship can be arbitrary. We feel a sense of solidarity with others even when we have no plan, when we are marching with placards just to express discontent with the status quo.

Yet this quest for kinship is not always healthy or useful, and it would seem that party politics is not currently fulfilling our need for engagement – in the UK, there have been sharply falling levels of membership in the major political parties (the total membership stood at just under 1 per cent of the population in 2018); hope and trust in these parties are fading fast. That may be a good thing, a necessary rejection of institutions and loyalties that are no longer fit for modern electorates. The British journalist Caitlin Moran put it well when she announced in her *Times* column of 5 April 2019 that, after many years of loyalty to the Labour Party, she was finally withdrawing her support, fed up with its ineptitude and infighting.

I now believe in no party. I have no faith. And I have to tell you, letting go of an old, heavy faith is wonderful. It is such a relief. I thought I would feel bereft or rootless. I thought I would lose a part of who I am. I thought I would have less interest in politics. But I have more now, now I'm not faithfully defending the current iteration of the party no matter what it does. A weight has been lifted – I don't have to spend hours, like some medieval monk, poring over scriptures to work out an interpretation of policy or statements that appear to support my own beliefs. I don't have to enter into conversations where I have to prove my faith to people who question if I'm a true believer.[3]

What she describes – the desperate and fruitless experience of trying to find meaning in an outdated relationship, the frustration with the petty battles that exist between opposing political parties – is not far from Thucydides' description of factions at work during civil war: 'Party associations are not based upon any established law nor do they seek the public good; they are formed in defiance of the laws and from self-interest.'

Perhaps political parties have a place in our democratic future, perhaps not. Perhaps we need radically new ones. But if we open up power to the masses in the way the ancient Athenians did, parties may not be necessary, just as they were unnecessary for the Athenians. If the future of democracy is constant referendums, this will not be compatible with representative democracy as we know it. We will need to allow voters to use their collective voice intelligently, rather than force them into giving yes–no answers to unclear questions.

It goes without saying that there are no quick fixes for democracy, and there are formidable odds to beat. Human behaviour at its worst is horrific and 'tramples laws underfoot', as

Thucydides noted so long ago, and we must take constant care to protect our democracy from ourselves – this is the way it has always been. To understand the trajectories of democracy, it can help to treat it as a paradigm for human behaviour, a sort of collective person – not in the wishful-thinking way that the Athenians did when they transformed Demokratia into a beautiful goddess to worship, but more realistically. Athens lost its nerve after losing the Peloponnesian War at the end of the fifth century BC; in the fourth century, it reacted more cautiously to threat, and became more conservative as a democracy – just as people often become more cautious after personal failure. We also know that power corrupts. Democracies will always behave badly away from home, when in control of people who are not in the system, just as people behave badly in an alien environment, freed from home etiquette.

It is a very Western form of arrogance for countries like Britain and the United States to believe they are inherently more civilized than democracies in the rest of the world. In April 2019, the Hansard Society published a sobering report on the British public's views on government; people had become so fed up with the government's mishandling of Brexit that 54 per cent of them would prefer a strongman leader, who would be 'willing to break the rules'. Looking at the global pattern of recent years – the elections of ex-reality-star Trump and the comedian Volodymyr Zelensky as president of Ukraine, the Brexit vote, and the rise of far-left and far-right parties across Europe – it does seem as though electorates across the world are rejecting traditional government in favour of something more radical.

People are imperfect, so it follows that democracy will always be imperfect – 'as long as human nature remains the same', as Thucydides predicted. But if people can spontaneously rally round to create democratic institutions, as they did in the fifth century BC, we can rally around to protect – and adapt – the democratic institutions we have today.

We have to.

Notes

1. 'On the Advantage and Disadvantage of History for Life', 1874.
2. *The Suppliant Women*, Aeschylus, 603−4, 607−609.
3. Thucydides, 1.22.
4. Hegel, *Philosophy of Right*, 1820.

Demokratia: The Life and Death of Ancient Democracy

1. Thucydides, 3.82−4.
2. *The Acharnians*, 19−22, translation by B. B. Rogers. William Heinemann, 1910, with adaptations.
3. A publicized text signed by the Union of Aesthetic Saboteurs of Antiquities.
4. Thucydides, 6.54 onwards.
5. Aristotle's *Athenian Constitution*, 18.6, translated Peter Rhodes, Penguin Classics, 1984.
6. St Augustine, *The City of God*, AD 426.
7. Aristotle's *Athenian Constitution*, 12, translated Peter Rhodes, Penguin Classics, 1984.

8. Thucydides, 2.37.
9. Aristotle's *Athenian Constitution*, 12, translated Peter Rhodes, Penguin Classics, 1984.
10. Aristophanes, *The Wasps*, 548–55.
11. Plato's *Apology of Socrates*, 28a, translated by Harold North Fowler; introduction by W. R. M. Lamb. Cambridge, MA, Harvard University Press; London, William Heinemann Ltd, 1966, with adaptations.
12. Erdoğan speaking at a meeting of Turkish ambassadors in Ankara on 12 January 2016.
13. 'Speech to the Electors of Bristol at the Conclusion of the Poll', delivered on 3 November 1774.
14. Thucydides, 3.43.

A Masterclass in Democracy from Ancient Athens

1. Thucydides, 2.40.
2. Euripides, *Hippolytus*, 421–3, translation our own.
3. Plutarch, *Themistocles*, 19.6.
4. Demosthenes, *On the Crown*, 169–70, translation by C. A. Vince, MA and J. H. Vince, MA. Cambridge, MA, Harvard University Press; London, William Heinemann Ltd, 1926.
5. Demosthenes, *First Olynthiac*, 6.20, translation by J. H. Vince, MA. Cambridge, MA, Harvard University Press; London, William Heinemann Ltd, 1930, with adaptations.
6. Horkheimer and Adorno's *Dialectic of Enlightenment*, first published 1944, English translation 1972 by John Cumming, New York, Herder and Herder.
7. Demosthenes, *First Olynthiac*, 19–20, translation by J. H. Vince, MA. Cambridge, MA, Harvard University Press; London, William Heinemann Ltd, 1930, with adaptations.

8. Lysias, 18.7, translation by W. R. M. Lamb, MA. Cambridge, MA, Harvard University Press; London, William Heinemann Ltd, 1930, with adaptations.

9. Thucydides, 6.16.

10. Xenophon, *Memorabilia*, 1.2.9, *Xenophon in Seven Volumes*, 4, translation by E. C. Marchant. Cambridge, MA, Harvard University Press; London, William Heinemann Ltd, 1923, with adaptations.

11. Karl Popper, *The Open Society and its Enemies*, vol. 1, *The Age of Plato*, Routledge, 1945.

12. 'Xenophon', *Ath. Pol*, 1, translation by J. L. Marr and P. J. Rhodes, *The 'Old Oligarch': The Constitution of the Athenians attributed to Xenophon*, Oxford, Aris & Phillips, 2008.

13. Ibid., 6–7.

14. Charles Mackay, *Extraordinary Popular Delusions and the Madness of Crowds*, Richard Bentley, 1841, p. xv.

15. Xenophon, *Hellenica,* 1.7.12, own translation.

16. Aristotle, *Politics*, Book 3, XI, translation by Daniela Cammack, with adaptations. 'Aristotle on the Virtue of the Multitude', Sage, 2013. https://www.academia.edu/2601792/Aristotle_on_the_Virtue_of_the_Multitude

17. https://brandfinance.com/news/lego-overtakes-ferrari-as-the-worlds-most-powerful-brand/

18. Peter Espersen, then-head of community co-creation at Lego Group, speaking at the Festival of Media 2014.

19. https://www.relationwise.com/blog/legos-customer-experience-told-brick-by-brick/

20. Thucydides, 3.37.

21. *The Wisdom of Crowds, Why the Many Are Smarter Than the Few and How Collective Wisdom Shapes Business, Economies, Societies and Nations*. Doubleday, 2004.

22. https://www.ch.ch/en/demokratie/political-rights/referendum/ mandatory-referendums-and-optional-referendums-in-switzerland/

23. James Fishkin and Bruce Ackermann, *Deliberation Day*, Yale University Press, 2005.

24. Neal Lawson, *Brexit Citizens Assembly: Rising to the United Kingdom's Crisis in Democracy*, Open Democracy, 9 December 2018. https://www.opendemocracy.net/en/opendemocracyuk/brexit-citizens-assembly-rising-to-crisis-in-democracy/

25. https://timesofindia.indiatimes.com/india/Will-take-a-56-inch-chest-to-turn-UP-into-Gujarat-Modi-to-Mulayam/articleshow/29269342.cms

26. http://time.com/4936612/donald-trump-genes-genetics/

27. https://edition.cnn.com/2016/03/01/politics/donald-trump-marco-rubio-beautiful-hands/index.html

28. https://www.bbc.com/news/av/world-europe-28530677/turkish-pm-Erdoğan-scores-football-hat-trick

29. https://www.cbsnews.com/pictures/vladimir-putin-doing-manly-things/24/

30. Thucydides, 2.65.

31. Plato, *Gorgias*, 515e−516c, *Plato in Twelve Volumes*, vol. 3, translation by W. R. M. Lamb. Cambridge, MA, Harvard University Press; London, William Heinemann Ltd, 1967, with adaptations.

32. Thucydides, 2.65.

33. Herodotus, 5.66, translation by A. D. Godley. Cambridge, MA, Harvard University Press, 1920, with adaptations.

34. Aristophanes, *The Knights*, 40.

35. Ibid., 46.

36. Ibid., 910.

37. Ibid., 255.

38. Ibid., 230.

39. Thucydides, 3.36.

40. https://www.whitehouse.gov/briefings-statements/
    remarks-president-trump-prime-minister-modi-india-joint-
    press-statement/

41. Demosthenes, *Third Olynthiac*, 30−31, translation by J. H.
    Vince, MA. Cambridge, MA, Harvard University Press;
    London, William Heinemann Ltd, 1930, with adaptations.

42. Lysias, 18.16, translation by W. R. M. Lamb, MA. Cambridge,
    MA, Harvard University Press; London, William Heinemann
    Ltd, 1930.

43. *Boris Johnson: The Incredible Rise*, BBC Two, 25 March 2013.

44. Philochorus, *Atthis*, translated by Philip Harding in *The Story
    of Athens: the Fragments of the Local Chronicles of Attika*, Rout-
    ledge, 2008.

45. *Metro*, 26 November 2018.

46. https://www.asa.org.uk/about-asa-and-cap/about-regulation/
    about-the-asa-and-cap.html

47. https://www.asa.org.uk/type/non_broadcast/code_section/03.
    html

48. https://twitter.com/JolyonMaugham/status/
    1110087443959742464

49. Demosthenes, 49.67, translation by A. T. Murray, PhD, LLD.
    Cambridge, MA, Harvard University Press; London, William
    Heinemann Ltd, 1939, with adaptations.

50. Speaking at the National Endowment for Democracy in
    2018. https://www.youtube.com/watch?v=OfIRfXJfrKE

51. Thucydides, 3.36 and following.

52. Herodotus, 1.133, translation by A. D. Godley. Cambridge,
    MA, Harvard University Press, 1920.

53. Thucydides, 6.15.

54. Thucydides, 6.9 and following.

55. Bodley Head, 2016.

56. Thucydides, 5, 111–13.

57. Speaking at the National Endowment for Democracy in 2018. https://www.youtube.com/watch?v=OfIRfXJfrKE

58. 'Shamima Begum's family v Sajid Javid: The letter in full', published 31 May 2019 in *The Times.*

59. Isocrates, 'Concerning the Team of Horses' speech 16. 46–47, translation by George Norlin PhD, LLD. Cambridge, MA, Harvard University Press; London, William Heinemann Ltd, 1980.

60. 'Was Athens a Democracy? Popular Rule, Liberty and Equality in Ancient and Modern Political Thought', Historisk-
filosofiske Meddelelser 59, Copenhagen, 1989.

61. Plutarch, *Life of Solon* 24.4, translation by Bernadotte Perrin. Cambridge, MA, Harvard University Press; London, William Heinemann Ltd 1914, with adaptations.

62. Aristotle, *Politics* 1275b.

63. https://www.timesofisrael.com/eu-states-increasingly-say-they-prefer-non-muslim-refugees/

64. https://www.independent.co.uk/news/world/europe/refugees-muslim-invaders-hungary-viktor-orban-racism-islamophobia-eu-a8149251.html

65. https://www.dw.com/en/slovakia-vows-to-refuse-entry-to-muslim-migrants/a-18966481

66. https://www.bbc.com/news/world-australia-47208915

67. From Attic Inscriptions Online (AIO), translated by Peter Rhodes. Ref: IG I³ 127.

68. https://www.migrationpolicy.org/programs/data-hub/charts/number-immigrants-who-became-us-citizens

69. IG II³ 1 337, From Attic Inscriptions Online (AIO), translated by Stephen Lambert.

70. Lucian, *Anarachsis*, translated by H. W. and F. G. Fowler. Oxford, The Clarendon Press, 1905.

71. https://twitter.com/KarlreMarks/status/199800591554318336

72. Herodotus, 4.76, translation by A. D. Godley. Cambridge, MA, Harvard University Press, 1920, with adaptations.

73. Lysias 12.20, *Against Eratosthenes*, translated by W. R. H. Lamb, in the Loeb Classical Library, 1930.

74. IG I³ 34, From Attic Inscriptions Online (AIO), translated by Stephen Lambert and Peter Rhodes.

75. https://edition.cnn.com/2018/07/10/politics/donald-trump-nato-summit-2018/index.html

76. https://twitter.com/realdonaldtrump/status/1016633811378073602?lang=en

77. Thucydides, 2.63.

78. IG I³ 40, From Attic Inscriptions Online (AIO), translated by Stephen Lambert and Robin Osborne.

79. Thucydides, 3.50.

80. IG I³ 14 (AIO 296), From Attic Inscriptions Online (AIO), translated by Stephen Lambert and Peter Rhodes

81. Thucydides, 3.82

82. https://twitter.com/qikipedia/status/1150751870886920192

Acropolis Redux: Ancient Democracy in a Digital Age

1. Report published by the European Commission in Brussels, 12 October 2011. https://eur-lex.europa.eu/legal-content/en/ALL/?uri=CELEX:52011SC1202

The Owl of Athena

1. http://www.xryshaygh.com/enimerosi/view/kophke-o-epitafios-tou-perikleous-ap

2. 'Destined for war? China, America and the Thucydides trap', article by Gideon Rachman published in the *Financial Times*, 31 March 2017.

3. 'I have lost my political faith', column by Caitlin Moran, *The Times*, 5 April 2019.

Select Bibliography

Dover, K. J. 1955. 'Anapsephisis in Fifth-Century Athens', *JHS* 75, 17−20.

Hansen, M. H. 1975. *Eisangelia*: the Sovereignty of the *People's Court in Athens in the Fourth Century* BC *and the Impeachment of Generals and Politicians*, Odense University Classical Studies, vol. 6.

——1991. *Athenian Democracy in the Age of Demosthenes*, Bristol Classical Press.

——1989. 'Was Athens a Democracy?', Royal Danish Academy for Sciences and Letters, vol. 59.

Harris, E. M. 2014. 'Nicias' Illegal Proposal in the Debate about the Sicilian Expedition (Thuc. 6.14)', *Classical Philology* 109, 66−72.

Knox, R. A. 1985. '"So Mischievous a Beaste"? The Athenian Demos and its Treatment of its Politicians', *G&R* 32, 132−61.

Κουμανούδης, Σ. Ν. (2nd ed. by Ματθαίου, Ἀ. Π. and Μπαρδάνη, Β. Ν. 1997. *Περιεκόπησαν τὰ πρόσωπα*, Athens.

Lewis, D. M. L. 1974. 'Entrenchment-clauses in Attic decrees' in D. W. Bradeen and M. F. McGregor (eds) *ΦΟΡΟΣ: Tribute to Benjamin D. Meritt* (Locust Valley, NY), 81−9 (*Selected Papers in Greek and Near Eastern History*, Cambridge 1997).

Marr, J. L. and Rhodes, P. J. 2008. *The 'Old Oligarch': The Constitution of the Athenians Attributed to Xenophon*, Aris & Philips Classical Texts.

Matthaiou, A. P. 2010. *The Athenian Empire on Stone Revisited*, Athens.

Osborne, M. J. 1981–3. *Naturalization in Athens*, vols 1–4, Brussels.

Rhodes, P. J. 1981 [1993]. *A Commentary on the Aristotelian Athenaion Politeia*, Oxford.

——1984. *Aristotle, The Athenian Constitution*, Penguin Classics.

——2009. *Athens in the Fourth Century BC*, Athens.

——2012. *Two Lectures on Athenian History*, Athens.

Sinclair, R. K. 1988. *Democracy and Participation in Athens*, Cambridge.

Surowiecki, James 2005. *The Wisdom of Crowds*.

Whitehead, D. 1977. *The Ideology of the Athenian Metic*, Cambridge Philological Society, supplementary volume no. 4.

Suggested Further Reading

Blok, J. 2017. *Citizenship in Classical Athens*, Cambridge University Press.

Camp, J. M. 2001. *The Archaeology of Athens*, Yale University Press.

Cartledge, P. 2016. *Democracy: A Life*, Oxford University Press.

Connor, W. R. 1971. *The New Politicians of Fifth-Century Athens*, Princeton University Press.

Finley, M. I. 1912 [1985]. *Democracy Ancient & Modern*, Rutgers University Press.

Fontaine, M. and Scafuro, A. (eds) 2014. *The Oxford Handbook of Greek and Roman Comedy*, Oxford Handbooks.

Forrest, W. G. 1966. *The Emergence of Greek Democracy: The Character of Greek Politics, 800–400 BC*, Weidenfeld and Nicolson.

Hignett, C. 1952. *A History of the Athenian Constitution to the End of the Fifth Century BC*, Oxford.

Jones, A. H. M. 1957. *Athenian Democracy*, Oxford, Blackwell.

Lang, M. 2004. *The Athenian Citizen. Democracy in the Athenian Agora*, Picture Book No. 4, ASCSA.

Samons II, L. J. 2007. *The Cambridge Companion to the Age of Pericles*, Cambridge University Press.

Ober, J. 1991. *Mass and Elite in Democratic Athens. Rhetoric, Ideology, and the Power of the People*.

Osborne, R. 1985. *Demos: The Discovery of Classical Attika*, Cambridge University Press.

Scott-Kilvert, I. 1960. *Plutarch, The Rise and Fall of Athens: Nine Greek Lives*, Penguin Classics.

Authors' Note

We are indebted to the following individuals for helping to shape this book: Robin Lane Fox for his encyclopaedic suggestions at the outset, Jeff Clackley for his brilliant translations of Aristophanes, Thucydides and Aeschylus, Mark Fisher for his advice on the subtleties of Thucydides, Matthew Scott for his legal eye, Bess Mayhew for her insights into modern deliberative democracy and Aris Mertilis for his unique illustrations. We are also grateful to the scholars Angelos Matthaiou and Peter Rhodes, as well as to the dedicated staff of the Epigraphical Museum of Athens and the British Archaeological School of Athens. The electronic resources of Attic Inscriptions Online (AIO), the Perseus Digital Library and PHI Searchable Greek Inscriptions have been invaluable to our work and to the work of others. Finally, thanks as ever to George Capel our wonderful agent, the unparalleled Jon Riley and Rose Tomaszewska at riverrun, and our friends and family for their contributions and support along the way.

Index

Page numbers in *italics* denotes an illustration